THE AUTOBIOGRAPHY OF
GUCCI

MANE

WITH NEIL MARTINEZ-BELKIN

SIMON & SCHUSTER

NEW YORK LONDON TORONTO SYDNEY NEW DELHI

Simon & Schuster
1230 Avenue of the Americas
New York, NY 10020

First Simon & Schuster hardcover edition September 2017

SIMON & SCHUSTER and colophon are registered
trademarks of Simon & Schuster, Inc.

For information about special discounts for bulk purchases,
please contact Simon & Schuster Special Sales at 1-866-506-1949
or business@simonandschuster.com.

The Simon & Schuster Speakers Bureau can bring authors to your
live event. For more information or to book an event, contact the Simon &
Schuster Speakers Bureau at 1-866-248-3049 or visit our website at
www.simonspeakers.com.

Interior design by Carly Loman

Manufactured in the United States of America

10   9   8   7   6   5   4   3   2

Library of Congress Cataloging-in-Publication Data

Names: Gucci Mane, 1980– author. | Martinez-Belkin, Neil.
Title: The autobiography of Gucci Mane / with Neil Martinez-Belkin.
Description: First Simon & Schuster hardcover edition. | New York : Simon &
   Schuster, 2017. | Includes index. | Description based on print version
   record and CIP data provided by publisher; resource not viewed.
Identifiers: LCCN 2017019427 (print) | LCCN 2017020490 (ebook) | ISBN
   9781501165337 (ebook) | ISBN 9781501165320 (hardcover : alk. paper) |
ISBN 9781501165344 (trade pbk. : alk. paper)
Subjects: LCSH: Gucci Mane, 1980- | Rap musicians—United States—
Biography.
Classification: LCC ML420.G9165 (ebook) | LCC ML420.G9165 A3 2017 (print) |
   DDC 782.421649092 [B] —dc23
LC record available at https://lccn.loc.gov/2017019427

ISBN 978-1-5011-6532-0
ISBN 978-1-5011-6533-7 (ebook)

For Walter Davis Sr., my maternal grandfather

&

Olivia Dudley, my paternal grandmother

CONTENTS

PART THREE

PROLOGUE

September 13, 2013

The police had taken my pistol the day before but I wasn't without heavy arms. I'd been stockpiling weapons at the studio. Glocks, MAC-10s, ARs fitted with scopes and hundred-round monkey nuts. All out in the open for easy access. I was in Tony Montana mode, bracing for a final standoff. I didn't know when it would happen, who it would be, or what would force its occurrence, but one thing I did know: something bad was going to happen and it was going to happen soon.

I looked around my studio. The Brick Factory. It seemed like just yesterday this had been the spot. Everybody would be over here. At all hours of the day for days on end. But now the Brick Factory looked more like an armory than a place where music was made. I'd seen the looks on people's faces when they came through. My studio was no longer a fun place to be. Onetime regulars started dropping like flies until I was the only one left. Alone.

Everyone was scared again. Not just scared of what was going on with me but scared *of* me. Scared to call me. Scared to see me. Keyshia had tried to be a voice of reason. She tried telling me the things I was stressing over weren't as bad as I was making them out to be. That my problems were manageable. That we could figure them out together. But I was too far gone and even Keyshia had her limits. A few days earlier I'd snapped on her and she'd hung up the phone. She'd had enough.

A paranoid mess, I went and checked the CCTV monitor for any activity outside. None. The parking lot was empty. The gate was secure. If that brought me any peace of mind, it disappeared as soon as I looked away from the screen, down at my feet.

The ankle monitor. I was a sitting duck. Everyone knew I was here. And they knew I couldn't leave.

That wasn't entirely true. I wasn't *supposed* to leave. But I had, the day before, when I'd gone to my lawyer Drew's office and the police got called. They found a loaded .45 next to my belongings. They let me go but took the strap with them to get fingerprinted and turned in to evidence. I knew my days were numbered. I'd violated my house arrest and had a run-in with the law while doing so.

Fuck it.

If I was going back to jail anyway, I might as well go find these niggas I'd been having problems with. These were my old partners, but things had soured and they'd been sending threats my way. I didn't want to wait until I got out of jail to see if these niggas were about all the shit they'd been talking. We could handle this now. I grabbed a Glock .40, some smoke, and was on my way.

During my walk to their spot I'd fallen into something of a trance, mumbling incoherent thoughts to myself as I wandered down Moreland Avenue. But my zombie-like state was interrupted by the red and blue flash of police lights. It immediately put me on high alert.

"Hi, Gucci," I heard. "I'm Officer Ivy with the Atlanta Police Department. What's going on?"

That was a red flag. No police had ever said "Hi, Gucci" to me like that before.

"Is everything okay? Your friends called us. They're worried about you."

Red flag number two. My friends were certified Zone 6 street niggas. They ain't the type to call the law.

None of this was adding up. Even with codeine and promethazine syrup slowing me down, my heart jumped as I realized what was happening. Or what I thought was happening. This man was no cop.

I knew niggas who did this. They'd dress up in police uniforms, get a kit put on their Dodge Chargers, and pull someone over, impersonating police. They'd tell them it was a routine traffic stop and before they knew it they were tied up in the trunk of their own car.

"Gucci, do you have any sort of weapon on you right now?"

"I do got a weapon," I barked back, pointing to the Glock bulging out of my jean pocket. "Don't unholster yours. I ain't surrendering nothing until you prove you're for real. Call for backup."

More officers arrived on scene but that didn't calm me. The standoff continued. When I told them I'd shoot 'em up if they touched me, they moved in and took me down, arresting me for disorderly conduct. After they found the gun and weed, more charges would follow.

Cuffed or not, I wasn't done fighting. I yelled, spat, and kicked as officers did their best to restrain me. Paramedics arrived and scrambled to inject me with a syringe. Were they poisoning me? When one wasn't enough they shot me up with another. Only then did I start to let up. I sank into the stretcher, a chemically induced calm putting an end to my nightmare.

August 14, 2014

Eleven months later I was in the US District Court of Georgia watching a conversation between Judge Steve Jones and Assistant US Attorney Kim Dammers. It was my sentencing hearing.

"... Nonetheless, the government thinks that this is in fact a just sentence. Mr. Davis has a substantial history of violence in the past. He has an aggravated assault in 2005 that's in paragraph twenty-nine in the presentence report, a battery that was also a probation—"

"I saw that," said Judge Jones.

"—in paragraph thirty-three. He has an aggravated assault pending in paragraph thirty-eight."

"I saw that."

"And of course there was the murder in DeKalb County that he was charged with but never brought to an indictment. And then there was also a battery in Henry County where the victims were unwilling to come forward. Reading between the lines, you could fairly say—"

"Violence."

"So given that, the government was not willing to enter in a low end of the guideline range. It's only two months' difference. It was more a matter of principle than anything, but I think thirty-nine months is a significant enough sentence for Mr. Davis to understand the seriousness of the offense."

A few minutes later Judge Jones was ready to make it official.

But before he handed down my punishment, he had some words for me.

"Mr. Davis, again, I want to explain to you why I'm accepting this binding thirty-nine months' confinement. You have a serious offense here. Possession of a firearm by a convicted felon is a serious offense and I think in looking at the 3553(a) factors, I have to take that into consideration, the history and characteristics of the defendant, and also deterrence. *You* are not supposed to have a firearm. I also look at the overall record and looking at everything—the factors and the presentence report—I find this to be an appropriate and reasonable sentence under the circumstances. Now, the sentence you are going to receive, the rest of it I'm going to tell you about in a minute . . .

"You are still a young man. You still have a full life in front of you. From what I've been told by my nieces and nephews, you have a very famous life. But I'm an old man and I've seen a lot of things in these years and I've seen a lot of famous people lose out in life. And I won't go down the list. I'm sure your lawyers can tell you who they are. I've seen a lot of famous athletes, a lot of famous people in music, movie stars. If they continue—if *you* continue down the track you continue down, you are going to be like a lot of them. You are going to wake up one morning broke. You are going to wake up one morning back in prison again. Or worse, you're not going to wake up at all one morning.

"You have a talent. Again I apologize, I'm still a Four Tops guy. It's hard to keep up. I've been trying to find out more things. According to my nieces and nephews you have a great career in front of you. You've got a prison term that you've got to do and after that you are still a young man. You can do a lot if you abide by and follow the law.

"The law applies to everybody. No matter who you are, what you do, the law applies to you. It applies to me. It applies to Ms. Dammers. It applies to the agents. To your attorneys Mr. Findling, Mr. Singer-Capek. Everybody in this room. You follow it, and again from what I've been told you have a lot you can get done."

Thirty-nine months. No surprises there. I'd agreed to it as part of a plea deal I'd accepted back in May.

While the judge, Ms. Dammers, and my lawyers went on to review the terms of my confinement and probation period, I started doing the math. A calculation I'd made a thousand times since they offered me that plea deal.

Thirty-nine months. I'd already served eleven, so that meant twenty-eight more. I could handle twenty-eight. Maybe only twenty-four if they let me serve the end of it on house arrest. Drew seemed certain we could make that happen. Twenty-four months. Two more years. Three total.

Give or take a few, thirty-nine months was about the amount of time I'd already spent locked up over the course of my life to date. But that time had been spread out over a series of different bids. Thirty-nine months straight up wasn't going to be easy. But I could get through it. And when I got out I'd still have some time to make things right.

When I did come home I'd have to start moving a different way. I was getting another chance but this was the last one. They were making an example out of me this time. Next time they were throwing away the key. No room to make the same mistakes.

Good. Things had to be different this time. I'd already started making changes. But I wasn't done. If I really wanted to start fresh I was going to have to find closure with everything that landed me here. Maybe I could do that in twenty-four months.

Talking about my life has not been easy. It's been that way for a long time, really ever since I caught that murder charge right as I was getting my start in the rap game. I remember walking out of DeKalb County Jail the day I made bond and seeing the line of reporters waiting for me. I wondered how long they would follow me. I wondered how long the events of that night would follow me. That was such a strange time.

I hated doing interviews. I'd try to keep my composure but inside I'd be festering, fuming that people were putting me in a situation where I had to speak on things that were the last things I wanted to speak about. I'd tell myself to give them the benefit of the doubt. That these were journalists doing their jobs. That they didn't know how fucked up it was to ask me those questions. That they weren't trying to disrespect me. Still, I always felt disrespected.

Over the years I tried to numb those feelings, to forget them, to pretend they didn't bother me. Didn't work. There are some things in life you can never completely walk away from, as badly as you might want to.

But I *could* try to make peace with all that had happened. And a lot had happened. Ups, downs, and all that led up to those ups and downs.

"Mr. Davis, is there anything you want to say before I sentence you?" Judge Jones said, bringing my attention back into his courtroom. "Anything you want to present?"

"I just want to first say that—"

"Stand up, please," he interrupted.

I stood up.

"I want to say that I thank you and I definitely don't want to withdraw my plea. I just thank you for your time."

"Okay. Thank you, Mr. Davis."

PART ONE

THE GUCCI MAN

I've got such strong ties to the city of Atlanta that people forget I didn't move to Georgia until I was nine.

My roots are in Bessemer, Alabama, a country coal town about twenty miles south of Birmingham. My great-grandparents on my daddy's side, George Dudley Sr. and Amanda Lee Parker, moved there in 1915 from the even more rural Greensboro, Alabama, where the Dudley family tree dates back to the 1850s.

George Sr. and Amanda headed to Bessemer in search of a better life. It was an area rich with natural resources—coal, limestone, ore—all the ingredients to sustain what was then a booming industry—steel. George Sr. managed to secure employment as an ore miner at the old Muscoda Red Ore Mining Company, near the community of Muscoda Village.

Back then steel companies looked out for their workers. Employees received cheap housing so most of the black miners of the mining community lived in company-owned homes. They created schools, a church, a medical dispensary, and a commissary where workers could purchase food and supplies on credit.

Soon enough white folk of the area turned jealous of the blacks' housing and the company-operated social programs, and decided they wanted them for themselves. So the blacks were moved out. Many were left homeless. But that wasn't the case for my great-grandfather. With the help of his money-minded wife he purchased a small home at 723 Hyde Avenue in Bessemer, a property that is family owned to this day.

George and Amanda had twelve children together—and 723 Hyde was bustlin'. Their household was a place where family and friends in need of a hot meal or a place to stay were always welcome. They were loving folks with big hearts.

When George Sr. would collect his paycheck, the stub would often be blank because of the money he owed the commissary for food. It never bothered him in the slightest.

George Sr. loved food—all the Dudleys did—and he loved to see his family eating right. He'd come home exhausted after a long day's work at the coal mine and still find the energy to cook something up for his family. And he'd always bring back a treat for his children—cookies, penny candy, fruits. He'd divide equally among all of 'em.

One of those twelve children was my grandfather James Dudley Sr., born April 5, 1920. James Sr. spent twelve years in the military as a cook and fought in the Second World War. After his time in the service he taught radio and television at Wenonah Technical School and later on worked as a postman.

James Sr. married Olivia Freeman on September 20, 1941.

They had eleven children, the sixth of whom was my father, Ralph Everett Dudley, born August 23, 1955.

Throughout the course of his life my father went by a lot of aliases. Slim Daddy. Ralph Witherspoon. Ricardo Love. For the purposes of this story, a nickname he received as a young boy matters most: Gucci Mane. That's right. He's the OG.

See, James Sr. had always fancied himself a dresser. He loved him some nice clothes and expensive leather shoes. He'd spent time in Italy during his years in the service, which is where he fell in love with the Gucci brand.

Originally he'd given the nickname Gucci to one of his nephews, an older cousin of my father's whom my father used to follow around all the time. Annoyed by his younger cousin always begging to hang and telling him "Come on, man," he started calling my father the "Gucci Man." As for how "man" became "Mane," well, I'm pretty sure that's just some country, Alabama twang. I've got an uncle on my momma's side they call Big Mane.

My auntie Kaye told me that as a boy my father was sharp, soft-spoken, and sensitive. He was always at the top of his class. He suffered from a speech impediment and would have to spell out words he was trying to say so people could understand him. James Sr., a military man, didn't always approve of his son's mild-mannered temperament, and would yell at him for refusing to fight with the boys in the neighborhood.

But as a young man my father came into his own. With his speech impediment gone he became a slick talker, very much a people person. He wore Levi's and played the guitar and listened to Jimi Hendrix, Peter Frampton, Mick Jagger—all the rock 'n' roll stars of the sixties and seventies. His bedroom had guitars mounted on the walls and tapestries hanging from the ceiling. He drove a two-seater drop-top convertible, an MG Midget. He was supercool, ahead of his time for a young black man from Alabama.

After graduating from Jess Lanier High School in 1973, my father enlisted in the US Army, spending two years stationed in South Korea. When he returned to Alabama in 1976, he briefly attended college before getting a job making dynamite at the Hercules Powder plant in Bessemer. After that he worked at the Cargill chemical plant. My father took full advantage of the GI Bill and had quite a bit of technical schooling under his belt. The guy was smart as hell.

But I never knew my father as a working man. I never saw him hold a nine-to-five job my whole life. All of that happened before me. I understood my father as a hustler, an alley cat, someone who more than any other person I've met was shaped by the streets. But I'm getting ahead of myself. More on all that later.

My momma's from Bessemer too. Vicky Jean Davis is the daughter of Walter Lee Davis. Walter and his siblings were raised not too far from Montgomery, Alabama, in Autauga County.

Walter was stationed in the Pacific during World War II, where he served aboard "Old Nameless," the battleship officially known as the USS *South Dakota*. He was a cook on Old Nameless, but when the Battle of Santa Cruz went down in October 1942, he hopped on one of the antiaircraft machine guns and got it poppin'. He took down a few planes before he got chewed up by one of the Japanese strafers. He got shot up so bad it made it into the papers.

"He looked like one of his own kitchen colanders," said the captain, Vice Admiral Tom Gatch. "But they couldn't kill him." It was a miracle he survived that battle.

When he came home Walter relocated to Bessemer, where he found employment at Zeigler's, a meat packaging company not unlike Oscar Mayer. He was one of their first black supervisors.

He also met his wife, Bettie. Together they had seven children—Jean, Jacqueline, Ricky, Patricia, Walter Jr., Debra, and Vicky. Bettie had two sons—Henry and Ronnie—from two prior marriages.

My momma's upbringing wasn't easy. Around the time of her birth Walter and Bettie took up drinking. Soon enough, violence became an everyday occurrence in the Davis household. To this day my family tells the craziest stories about my grandmomma. Bettie Davis was a mean drunk like you wouldn't believe. This little lady would get to fighting with somebody at dinner and reach across the dining room table and stab them with a fork. Hell, I heard she shot my granddaddy once.

When she passed away from a stroke at the young age of forty-four, my mother's sisters had to take on the role of caretaker for their younger siblings. They kept a roof over everyone's head and food on the table, but there was a lot to be desired. My aunties were only a few years older than my momma and they hadn't had the best role models themselves.

But as resilient people do, my momma adapted to survive. Vicky Davis always was, and to this day remains, a very smart, hardworking, resourceful woman. And tough. She graduated from Jess Lanier High School in 1975 and went on to get an associate's degree at Lawson State. After Lawson she enrolled in Miles College, a historically black school in Fairfield, Alabama, where she studied to become a social worker.

That's around the time she met Ralph Dudley, in 1978. My father already knew the Davis family. He'd been classmates with my aunt Pat at Lanier. But he'd never met my momma. When he did it was instant attraction. They fell in love quick.

My momma already had a son, my older brother, Victor. He goes by Duke. But Duke's father wasn't in the picture. Duke's got another half brother, Carlos, who was born the same month and year he was. So that's what his daddy was up to then.

During my momma's pregnancy my father got into trouble with the law. He'd been arrested for having drugs on him—no small crime in the seventies—and was facing time. James Sr. had recently passed away unexpectedly and my grandmother Olivia—whom we call Madear—still had kids to raise. So instead of facing the music, which would cause Madear the undue stress of seeing her son sent to prison, my father fled.

He headed north to Detroit, which was where he was on the day of my birth, February 12, 1980.

Because my father wasn't around to sign the birth certificate I was born Radric Delantic Davis, taking my mother's last name. Like my conception nine months before, my first name, Radric, was a product of my parents' union—half Ralph, half Vicky.

II

1017

I came up in my granddaddy's house at 1017 First Avenue—an olive-green, two-bedroom in Bessemer near the train tracks. Inside were my granddaddy, my momma, Duke, and me. But it was never just us.

1017 had a rotating cast of family characters who could be staying there at any time. Walter Jr., my uncle—we call him Goat—was always in and out of jail. When he wasn't locked up, he'd be there. Or one of my many aunties and her kids might move in for a while.

The house was small, 672 square feet to be precise, so things got tight. Sometimes Duke and I got the bunk beds. Sometimes I'd be on the couch. Other times the floor. My granddaddy had an extra roll-away bed in his room. At one point there was a bed in the living room. It switched up.

Growing up, I called Walter Sr. Daddy. He and I were close.

Tall and slender, my granddaddy appeared every bit the gentle-man. He wore a suit and tie every day. On Saturdays one of my cousins would go to the cleaners and pick up his freshly pressed clothes for the week. They'd grab him cigarettes too. This was back when kids could buy cigarettes. Camel Straights.

My granddaddy and I had this thing where I would see him up the block coming home from the First Baptist church. As soon as I'd see him turn the corner I'd stop playing kickball or football or whatever it was I was doing and race up First Avenue to meet him. I'd grab his hand and help him walk the rest of the way home.

"Your grandson sure loves you, Mr. Walter," the old ladies would call out from their porches.

The funny thing was my granddaddy didn't need help walk-ing. His cane had gotten himself to church just fine. But he played along, putting on a limp like he needed my help. That was our inside thing and I felt proud to walk alongside him.

Like many in my family, he had his demons. I don't know if my granddaddy turned to the bottle to cope with the men-tal or physical effects of war. Deep scars crossed his body. Or maybe it was something invisible. Whatever it was, the man was a drinker.

In Bessemer most folks drank the wino wines—Wild Irish Rose, Thunderbird—but my granddaddy liked liquor. Bourbon. He had a girlfriend, Miss Louise, and the two of them would get pissy drunk at one of the shot houses nearby until they were stumbling down the street with bloodshot eyes.

But I loved my granddaddy. Every night I would sit on his knee and we'd watch TV. When I would act up he'd chase me around the house, saying he was gon' whip me, and I'd dive under his bed laughing, knowing that he couldn't catch me down there.

I was just as close with Madear, my grandmother on my father's side. She'd played a big part in my childcare while my momma was in college working toward her degree.

Madear's house was over in Jonesboro Heights, an even quieter, even more country part of Bessemer that sits on a hill outside the city limits. It's a tight-knit community made up of three streets—Second Street, Third Street, and Main Street—with two churches: New Salem Baptist and First Baptist. It's known fondly by its residents as the Happy Hollow.

As soon as I learned to ride a bicycle I struck out on my own to go there. I'd get in trouble for doing that. It wasn't like the Hollow was around the corner. It was a ways away. You had to cross the main highway to get there. For a little boy, the mile-and-a-half trek was a real journey. But I loved spending time with Madear. She spoiled me.

Whenever I'd come over she'd have something for me—toys, coloring books, GI Joes. We'd watch TV for hours. Sometimes wrestling, sometimes *Wheel of Fortune*, sometimes *Jeopardy!*

"There's my smart grandbaby," she'd say if I knew the answer to one of the trivia questions. "I don't even have to think anymore because I know Radric knows the answers."

If I wasn't with one of my grandparents, then I was following my brother around. Duke is six years older, so you know how that goes. To me he was supercool, and I was his shadow. I really got on his nerves. I would always be stealing his clothes to wear and trying to hang with him and his buddies.

Duke didn't care for that much, but I didn't care that he minded. I'd trail him and his little crew on my bike, usually from a distance because my brother would beat my ass if he knew I was following them. He didn't want me to see what he and his friends were up to. I'd watch them steal beers from the corner store or throw rocks through car windows and take off running. It wasn't much. Country teenagers getting into country teenage shit. But I was a curious child. I needed to know what everyone was up to.

Duke was a bona fide music enthusiast. He put me onto all the great hip-hop of the eighties. Every week he would go to the Bessemer Flea Market and come home with whatever new album had just come out. He'd pop the cassette in his boom box and we would listen to the albums endlessly. We'd focus on the lyrics, committing them to memory. Then we'd start rapping to each other, alternating verses.

Even when Duke wasn't around I would listen to his tapes on my own. Actively, carefully, diligently. Damn near studying them.

Duke brought me to my first concerts at the Birmingham Civic Center. The summer of 1986 I saw Run-DMC, the Beastie Boys, Whodini, and LL Cool J on the Raising Hell Tour. I was six years old. That shit blew my mind. Two summers later I saw Kool Moe Dee, Eric B. & Rakim, Doug E. Fresh, Boogie Down Productions, Biz Markie, and Ice-T on the Dope Jam Tour. What a lineup. When Kool Moe Dee dropped "Let's Go," his diss going at LL Cool J, the whole arena went crazy. In 1989 I saw N.W.A perform there. That was the concert after which MC Ren was accused of raping a girl on their tour bus.

The bedroom Duke and I shared was covered with posters of all these guys he'd pulled out of *Word Up!* magazine. Top to bottom. His favorite was one with LL and Mike Tyson on it. You couldn't see a speck of the room's wall, there were so many posters.

•

From time to time my father would slip into Alabama. We looked forward to those visits. He would pull up in a clean, white Cadillac—a Fleetwood Brougham with white leather interior. He was tall, six-four, and slim. He would step out of the car bearing gifts; clothes and toys for me and Duke and a bankroll for my momma. Back then we always knew my father to have some money on him. To me the guy was rich as hell.

As a child I was told my father was a lab technician, which at some point had been true. But by the time I was born those days were far gone.

"Oh, he's a lab technician?" Madear laughed when I said it. "So tell me, what does he wear to work?"

How was I supposed to know what he wore to work? I hardly knew the man.

The closest thing I had to a father passed when I was seven. Duke and I were in the house when Goat rushed in, carrying Walter Sr. in his arms. He'd collapsed in the street.

I had witnessed similar scenes earlier. I said before that my granddaddy could walk just fine but not when he got drunk. I'd see him falling into the ditch that ran along our street. My uncle or one of the neighbors would scoop him up and usher him into the house. Honestly that was a normal occurrence.

But this time was different. This time was a heart attack. This time was the last I'd see Walter Sr. Goat brought him into the bedroom and closed the door. By the time the paramedics arrived he was gone.

The next day the whole Davis family arrived. It was something else. Hysteria. At the funeral my momma and my aunties were cuttin' a fool, jumping up and down, crying and screaming like they were fittin' to climb up in the casket with him. It was a real scene.

"Why, Lord, why?"

My grandfather's passing marked the beginning of the end of my life in Bessemer. It wasn't more than a few hours after the funeral that the Davis family was at odds. This fighting, primarily among the women, would go on for years. On the surface the conflict was over Walter Sr.'s house. But it went deeper than that. It was a power struggle over who was the new matriarch. And my momma was pitted against her two older sisters, my aunties Jean and Pat.

Listen, when I say that my momma and aunties got to fighting, I mean there was blood, on multiple occasions. This shit would be like a saloon fight, spilling onto the front lawn for all the neighbors to see.

One night my momma pushed Aunt Jean through the front window. Another time Aunt Pat came through with a can of gasoline, hollering about how she was going to burn the house down. Things got so bad that my momma took Duke and me to her friend's house just so we could get away from the chaos.

In the midst of the bickering and fighting my momma became more involved in the church. Prior to this religious awakening, Vicky Davis smoked cigarettes and I think even weed on occasion. I've heard she even sold some weed. But all that stopped after she got saved. She even stopped cussing.

With all that was going on with the family, my momma got it in her head that she wanted to get us out of Alabama. Life in Bessemer didn't get much better than finding a job at Pullman-Standard, the railroad car company that paid more than anywhere else. That was all there really was to aspire to. The ceiling was low. She wanted more. For herself, for me, for Duke.

At the time, my momma had a boyfriend who would travel back and forth to Atlanta for work. He'd once taken us all out there to Six Flags. One day my momma told Duke and me that we were moving to Atlanta with him. Pretty soon our stuff was packed up and out on the curb, ready to go. But the guy never showed.

It would take nearly a year before we actually made the move. Through church my momma met another man, Donald. Donald always struck me as a nice guy, very much a churchgoing man. He drove truck for a living. My understanding was that he and my momma were just friends, but he was planning on moving back to Georgia, and because he knew about our tumultuous family situation, he invited us along. We would stay at his house while my momma looked for a job and got her money right.

I didn't know what to think when my momma told us for the second time we were moving. Duke was still embarrassed from when we got stood up, so he wasn't paying it any mind this time around. He didn't tell his football coach or his friends that he was leaving. He didn't pack up his things. So neither did I. Sure enough, Donald showed up.

Duke wasn't happy. My brother had a life in Alabama and he had plans there too. All Duke ever wanted was to play Alabama Crimson Tide football and go on to the pros. To follow in Bo Jackson's footsteps and be the next star athlete to make it out of Bessemer. He didn't want to leave and he didn't understand why we had to.

But I did. As much as I loved my aunties and my cousins, it was troubling to have everybody fighting the way they was. It was no way to live. Even at nine years old I thought it was so stupid how these grown folks were fighting so hard over this rickety little house. It was crazy to me.

Everybody from our street came outside to see us off the day we left for Georgia. It was a big deal for us to leave Bessemer. Nobody in that town just up and moved. This was a community of families who'd lived there for generations.

As the U-Haul pulled off I waved good-bye to family and friends as they chased the truck.

Wow. I'll probably never see any of these folks again.

III

WELCOME TO ATLANTA

We arrived in Ellenwood, Georgia, in August 1989.

Ellenwood is a suburb a few miles outside of Atlanta. It didn't seem that different from my community back in Bessemer. Folks hung out on their porches to escape the heat. Squirrels and rabbits ran through people's yards. Children played outside and rode their bikes without fear of something happening to them. It felt familiar. But our time in Ellenwood wouldn't last long.

A few months after the move Donald reconciled with his ex-wife and she and their son moved into the house with us. Donald was a decent guy and as far as I know he never told my momma we had to leave. But from the day his wife moved in it was clear she did not want us there. One day she tore down all of Duke's posters that he'd brought from Bessemer and threw them in the trash. My brother was heartbroken.

This lady and my momma couldn't share a home. Small arguments turned big. It wasn't long before my momma wanted out.

Problem was we had nowhere to go. My momma had no idea where to move us nor did she have the means to get us there. We were brand-new to Georgia. No family, no friends, no support system.

We knew my father was somewhere nearby. After fleeing Alabama for Detroit, he'd settled down in Atlanta, where his older brother, my uncle James Jr., put him up until he found a spot of his own. But he and my momma hadn't spoken in some time. A year or two back my momma found out my father met another woman and that he had two other boys—my half brothers, Ralph and Courtney Walker. That news put an end to his visits to Bessemer.

But we were desperate. So my momma got ahold of Madear, who sent my father to Ellenwood to get us. He came right away. He couldn't wait to see us; it had been my momma who hadn't wanted him around. We moved our things into a storage unit and my father put us up in a Knights Inn motel on Bouldercrest Road on the Eastside of Atlanta. It was here that I began to get acquainted with the city that would shape me.

•

Atlanta's drug trade is tied to its roots as a railroad town. The city quickly became the primary transit hub of the Southeast, with rail lines that ran north, east, south, and west of it. Even after the railroads were destroyed during the Civil War, Atlanta's identity as a mecca of transport lived on. The rails were replaced by a web of interstate highways connecting cities in every direction. A Spaghetti Junction. Long story short, Atlanta's got a history of moving people and things. Drug trafficking is a natural part of that history.

When crack hit in the mideighties, it hit Atlanta hard. A crew out of South Florida called the Miami Boys were behind a lot of the dope flooding into Atlanta's projects. But by the time I arrived, those guys were on their way out. The city was working hard to land the '96 Olympic Games and increase tourism. To do that, Atlanta had to deal with its reputation as unsafe and drug-ridden. So the Miami Boys had to go. The feds came in and took them out.

But that didn't fix anything. Taking one big gang out just made room for the smaller ones to step up. When they did, they clashed. The violence continued. The drugs continued. Same shit, different toilet.

The folks at city hall couldn't accept that. Atlanta needed the Olympics. So as part of the efforts to downplay the city's dark underbelly, the police department started underreporting crime. Violent crimes were downgraded to misdemeanors and other police reports were being thrown away altogether. This went on for years.

But enough playing dope-game historian. Because I didn't know about any of that shit then. I was ten years old. All I knew was my new neighborhood was a fucking drug zone. Zone 6.

The Knights Inn was infested with dope as was the rest of the Eastside. Deals were being made in the middle of traffic in broad daylight. Prostitutes on every corner. The robbing crew always out looking for the next stickup. It was very, very rough.

There were also a lot of rumors going around about children being kidnapped, molested, and murdered. It had been ten years since the Atlanta Child Murders, where nearly thirty black boys and adults had been abducted and killed, but the story still loomed large over Atlanta families. A lot of folks seemed to think Wayne Williams wasn't the only killer, if he was even the killer at all.

For a young boy from the country, all of this was frightening. Culture shock. My new surroundings were so aggressive. The people in it seemed vicious. Cruel.

After spending almost a year at the Knights Inn, the four of us moved to Mountain Park, an apartment complex on Custer Avenue made up of redbrick low-rises. A little nicer than the motel but essentially the same shit.

We were now living in East Atlanta, but Duke and I were still going to school by Ellenwood. I was at Cedar Grove Elementary and Duke was at Cedar Grove High. Cedar Grove had a good football program and like I said earlier my brother was a hell of a ball player. He mostly played linebacker but you could put him anywhere on the field. Hell, Duke could even punt. He later got a scholarship to play ball at Tennessee Wesleyan University. I imagine he was supposed to go to a different high school after we moved to East Atlanta, but somehow he got to stay at Cedar Grove to play ball, which meant that I got to stay at my school too.

•

Since kindergarten back in Alabama, school had been easy for me. Because my momma was a teacher, she'd taught me how to read young, and I took to it quickly. At Sunday school the teachers were in awe that I was able to read and recite scripture from the Bible. So when I did enroll in kindergarten at Jonesboro

Elementary I was way ahead of my peers. I finished my work before anyone else. I was praised for being a good student but I knew it was because my momma had given me a head start. I carried over that early advantage as I continued my education in Atlanta.

Like my brother, I was naturally athletic, but I never had his drive and ambition when it came to sports. It didn't interest me. I never wanted no letterman jacket. I envisioned myself as the guy at school with a nice car. The guy who dressed the best. The one with a bankroll in his pocket. As far back as I can remember, I really just wanted to get me some money.

•

The move to East Atlanta had instilled in me a deep financial fear. It seemed like every month my momma was saying we were behind on the rent, or we didn't have money to pay the light bill. I'd eavesdrop on her calls and hear her telling my aunties in Bessemer that shit just wasn't going right for us. I was seeing people in the neighborhood get evicted—something you didn't see in Alabama—and I became convinced that would be our fate.

That I was still going to school in Ellenwood only made me feel poorer. The kids at Cedar Grove were by no means rich, but they came from working-class families and their houses were definitely nicer than our Mountain Park apartment or the Knights Inn motel.

I grew up thinking my father had money, but once we got up with him in Georgia I realized that wasn't the case, at least not anymore. I discovered that back in the day, my father sold heroin and coke, but by the time he entered my life in Atlanta he was a full-fledged con artist. Every penny he made came by way of tricking somebody else out of theirs.

Not long after he left Alabama my father made friends with a guy named Tony from Philadelphia. He'd taught Tony the ins and outs of the dope game and in return Tony put him onto the con game. Three-card Molly, pigeon drop, shaking the pea—all sorts of trickery and bullshit.

To my father everyone was a potential mark. He couldn't turn it off. He had to beat everybody. We might pull up to Hardee's on Bouldercrest to get cheeseburgers and he'd hand the cashier a fifty-dollar bill. They'd give him his change, and with a quick sleight of hand he'd swap it out with some lesser amount he'd had ready to go for that exact moment.

"Excuse me, ma'am?"

When my father got to talking all proper like that you knew somebody was about to get got.

"Ma'am, you must have miscounted my money. I gave you a fifty-dollar bill."

It worked every time. He might only make a couple of dollars off something like that, but it worked every time.

I learned a lot being around my father. He taught me all his little tricks, but what he was really teaching me was how to size people up, how to read body language, and how to use that information for my benefit. Everything about the man was smooth. Even his hands, they were softer than my momma's. And he had so many different sayings. I got so much slang from Gucci.

Empty wagon make the most noise.

If you keep lookin' back, you gon' trip going forward.

Buddy eat shit and bark at the moon.

Three things I never seen: a flying saucer, a pigeon in a tree, or a nigga or a bitch I need.

Most niggas cross the street, I cross the country. If I get enough cheese I will cross the continent. From Maine to Spain, I can play that thang, because I'm the original Gucci Mane.

As sick as he was, my father's tricks weren't paying the bills. When he'd first gotten to Atlanta in the early eighties he and his crew hit the city hard with the cons. People in Georgia weren't familiar with Three-card Molly, so they tore the town up. But that hustle started to dry up. Folks weren't falling for that shit anymore. The days of white Cadillacs were over.

Even when he did stumble into money, it was never long before he lost it gambling in the streets. Gambling was his vice. One of them.

You could *feel* it when Gucci came into some money. He'd stroll into the apartment and it would be like a breath of fresh air came in. He was generous and would share the wealth, bringing us gold chains, watches, and rings. All kinds of different jewelry he'd tricked off somebody or won in a dice game.

But when he was broke, and that was more often than not, things were tense. He came home from the Kentucky Derby one year—an annual pilgrimage he made—and he had like twenty thousand dollars he'd made tricking folks and betting on the horses. It was a celebration. A few days later that money was gone.

His other vice was the sauce. My father got drunk every day. Morning, noon, night. Before he'd even leave the house he'd put down a pint of cheap gin. He'd chase it with a sip of water, swish it around in his mouth, and spit into the sink. I remember the sound. The bottles would get thrown away but he would keep the caps. He used those for the pea game. Then he'd head out, taking the MARTA bus downtown to find people to con. He'd be drunk as hell by the time he got home at night, reeking of alcohol.

All of that was a reality check. I learned young that if I ain't got shit, then I just ain't got shit. If I wanted something in life, I would have to find a way to get it myself. Constantly worrying about money the way that I did messed me up. I would tell myself when I got grown I'd never live with those feelings. Twenty-five years and millions of dollars later I still remember that anxiety.

My first enterprise was picking up aluminum cans in the neighborhood and taking them down to the store for a few cents each. That's how I met my friend OJ, who would become the rapper OJ da Juiceman. OJ was a few years younger than me and he lived in Mountain Park too. Together we'd canvass the hood for cans. Sometimes we'd save time by stealing bags of cans that had already been collected by the older guys in the neighborhood. We'd hop their fences, grab the bags from the yard, and take off running.

But the real way I started to make money was selling drugs. I was in the seventh grade. At the time Duke was rolling with some of the hustlers in the neighborhood. These were the niggas driving fixed-up cars, who had the sickest gear, and were known for carrying weapons. I never had no positive male role models growing up so to me, these were the coolest guys I knew. My brother would never go full-on in the streets like me, but back then he was selling a little bit of weed.

Duke selling weed was his way of keeping up with the niggas he was running with. Duke was never really a hustler. His passion was football. Plus he had a job at the Winn-Dixie grocery store, so he really didn't have much time to be hustling. So he eventually put me onto his package. I would serve his boys who would want weed for themselves or somebody else they knew. From the jump, the shit was fun to me.

Duke's friends used to call me "worker," as in my brother's little worker. I hated being called that, but I couldn't fight these dudes because they were six years older than me. It made me resent my brother because I felt like he was playing me to his buddies. I wanted to find a way to pull one over on him and be my own man.

Here was the deal. Duke would give me thirty dollars on every hundred I brought in. What he didn't know was that of the ten ten-dollar dime sacks he gave me, I was pinching out of each one to make an extra sack. I'd sell his ten sacks and make thirty dollars, then sell the extra one and make ten dollars more. When the time came for me to turn over four hundred dollars, Duke was thinking I'd made $120 when really I'd made $160. That was my father in me. Always looking for the angle. Always thinking about what move I could pull to my advantage, however small that move might be.

•

It wasn't long after I began selling weed for Duke that I endeavored to start my own operation. That came about during the Christmas break from school of my eighth-grade year.

Coming back after break was like the first day of school. Everybody would show up with their new toys, clothes, sneakers—whatever stuff they'd gotten from Santa. That year I had my eyes on some jeans, some Jordans, and a Starter jacket. But as Christmas neared my momma told me she wouldn't be able to get me any of it.

"Bills are really tight right now, Radric," she told me. "I'm sorry I can't get you this stuff. I promise I'll get it for you later."

I couldn't go back to school with the same old shit on while everybody else was fresh as hell. I just couldn't. I tried to explain but my momma cut me off.

"Look, here's fifty dollars," she told me. "Get whatever you want."

What the hell was I supposed to do with fifty dollars? I couldn't buy that Starter for fifty dollars. I couldn't get a pair of Jordans for fifty dollars. I couldn't get any of the things I wanted.

Frustrated, I took the money and left the apartment, walking toward the other side of Mountain Park. I knew that's where the dope man stayed. I handed him the money and he handed me two tightly wrapped fifty-dollar slabs of crack cocaine.

"Now you owe me fifty dollars, get it?" he said.

I sure did.

That was all she wrote.

The dope game was on and poppin' from that moment on. There would never be any other sort of extracurricular activities for me again.

DOPE GAME HARD

Even though I brought the fifty dollars to the dope man like I'd done a thousand times before, I had no idea what I was getting into. It wasn't like with the weed, where I was getting dime bags already packaged and serving my brother's friends. I was on my own with this dope shit. This was a totally different kind of product with a totally different type of clientele.

I had a buddy who knew more about dope than I did and he helped me cut up those slabs the first few times I picked up.

A fifty-dollar bag of crack was roughly 1.5 grams. That got broken down into twenty-dollar bags, ten-dollar dime bags, and five-dollar nickel bags. You could make a little more or a little less depending on how you played it, but most of the time there was a hundred-dollar return on a fifty-dollar slab. Then you go get you a hundred-dollar slab. Profit.

My buddy also knew a place where I could get a few of these

sacks off. He brought me to a run-down house on Custer where we were greeted by an old lady with salt-and-pepper hair who introduced herself as Miss K. She was a nasty-looking woman, gangly thin with sores all over her face and body.

Her home was even more disgusting than she was. This spot was a smoking house for junkies and truck drivers, but she also had ladies in there selling pussy. All sorts of foul shit going down. There were little kids running around and rotting food littered everywhere. I'd never seen anything like it.

The deal with Miss K was that she'd give me the green light to serve her people, but I had to hook her up with a sack free of charge. A finder's fee. That was a fair enough deal, except I was so shook by the scene that I fumbled a few sacks on my way out. This happened on more than one occasion, to the point that Miss K told my buddy that I needed to tighten up and get my shit together. She could see how rattled I was, that I didn't want to touch anything in there. But it wasn't long before I grew numb to that environment. I went on to serve Miss K and her folks for years. I didn't give a fuck about her sores or that house of horrors anymore. I was making money.

I took to the dope game quickly. I got creative with it. Innovative. When other niggas went from selling dimes to selling nicks, I started selling three-dollar sacks. My margins were slimmer but I was selling out quicker. The junkies were buying them and then selling to each other for five dollars. I saw those three-dollar sacks as an investment. I was building my reputation along with my business.

Hiding my activities from my momma was easy. It wasn't that she didn't care, and I wouldn't call her naive either. I would just say she worked a lot and I wasn't giving her any reason to question my whereabouts. Besides the occasional fistfight, I was never a troublemaker at school and I'd stayed bringing home good grades. I was now a freshman at Ronald E. McNair High School on Bouldercrest and I was popular. It was never hard to get someone to let me copy their homework.

When my momma did get suspicious I was always a step ahead of her. I'd picked up a thing or two watching my father bullshit so many people.

I remember when she first noticed I had come into some money. I came home one day with a seven-hundred-dollar leather 8-ball jacket. I told her I won some money in a tunk game with my father. That wasn't that far-fetched, because he did let me shoot dice and get in on the card games with his crew.

Eventually my momma caught me red-handed, finding sacks of dope in my jeans when she was doing the laundry.

"Momma, you know that guy who be washing your car, cutting the grass, and taking out the trash for us?"

"Black?"

"Yeah, well Black don't be doing all that for free," I said. "And he said he wants this stuff. He don't want no money."

My momma knew Black was a J and she knew dope was everywhere in Mountain Park. The idea that someone had given this to me and I was passing it on to Black wasn't that hard to believe. Even if it was, I knew my momma liked Black. Junkie or not, he was a part of the community. And she definitely liked having her car washed and the trash taken out, so I was off the hook. No further questions. With my momma off my back and my father out doing whatever it was he was up to, I was free to make plays.

By fifteen I'd been selling weed and dope for a few years

but I still hadn't used myself. My early experiences with Miss K and the neighborhood crackheads had been a deterrent. I'd interacted with countless fiends and they were so fucked-up and broke it turned me off to the idea of getting high. My buddies had been pressing me to smoke weed for years but I'd resisted. As a hustler I felt above using. It seemed lame to me. Plus I wasn't about to let my friends peer-pressure me.

But one day I was walking up to the gas station when I saw this girl who had moved into the apartments. She was a couple of years older than me at McNair. She was the talk of the hood. Fine as hell. She had on tight black spandex shorts, standing outside of her apartment and was talking on a cordless phone.

I was eying her when a car drove up and flagged me down. I served them and took my time doing so. I wanted her to know I was a hustler.

After they pulled off I approached her and asked if I could use her phone. I called my trap back and was talking about all the moves I'd made that day. I was showing out. When I hung up she was standing there looking at me.

"You smoke?" she asked.

"Of course I smoke," I lied. "Let me go get a blunt."

I ran up to the gas station. When I got back I placed the Swisher and a bag of weed on the coffee table.

"So . . . are you gonna roll it?" she asked.

Not only had I never smoked, I'd never rolled a blunt either and I'd only picked up one. There was no room for error. Luckily I rolled that shit like a pro and fired it up, taking a deep pull like I'd seen folks do.

I've heard people say you don't get high the first time you smoke, but it hit me instantly. I was high as hell. This was some powerful shit and I was trippin', overwhelmed, paranoid, all that. But the girl got me something cold to drink and we sat down; after a couple of minutes I calmed down. Hell, I was actually feeling pretty good. I liked being high.

That girl became my smoking buddy. I still didn't want my buddies to know I smoked, so she was the only person I did it with. She'd hit me on my beeper and I'd walk to her spot and we'd burn one down. After a few weeks of that we started fucking too, so it became a good little arrangement. We never ended up having a relationship or anything, but she was cool.

•

Trapping had been nothing but fun for me since day one. I felt cool, I was making money, and I'd never had problems with the law. But the dope game stopped being a game the day I got robbed.

I'd seen him earlier. I had reupped with my plug, and as I was leaving his trap house this older nigga pulled up on me. I recognized him from the neighborhood. Nobody liked this guy. He was a bully and a known robber.

"Hey, little buddy. What you be buying? Fifty slabs?" he asked me. "Fuck with me, I'll front you one extra if you buy from me."

"Thanks, but I'd rather deal with my own people," I said, walking away.

Hours later I was by the car wash on Custer. I was on my bike and had just served some niggas. As I turned to peddle away I glimpsed something out of the corner of my eye. It was a .45 Desert Eagle handgun pointed at my head. It was the dude from earlier.

"Give me everything."

I had four hundred dollars' worth of dope tucked in my ass crack, but even with that big pistol in my face, my only thought was the consequences of giving up my stash.

If I give him my bomb, I'm not going to have anything.

I emptied my pockets and handed over the contents: a bag of weed, forty dollars cash, and a few sacks of dope. But I kept that slab clenched tight between my ass cheeks.

He'd been watching me all day. He saw me catch a trap and leave the house of a drug dealer. That's why he targeted me. He could have easily blown my ass off right then and there for lying, but for some reason he didn't. He just left.

I biked back to my plug's spot and told him what happened. Well, not exactly what happened.

"I just got robbed," I said. "He took everything, the whole bomb I just got from you."

"It's cool, man," he told me. "Just don't fuck with that guy. That's the type of nigga who will *actually* kill you."

He went on to give me another four hundred dollars' worth of dope because he felt bad. So I turned that bad situation to my benefit. Now I was up four hundred dollars.

Still, I was far from happy about the episode. Getting robbed shook me up. Ever since I'd moved to East Atlanta I'd seen plenty of kids in the hood get jumped and have their shit snatched, but not once had that happened to me. I think a lot of those older stickup boys spared me because they were cool with my brother. But I knew then I couldn't depend on that anymore. All bets were off.

When I came home that night I told Duke. He wasn't keen on how deep I was getting in the streets, but we were in agreement that I needed to be able to protect myself. I needed to get me a strap. Duke didn't sell dope but even he kept a pistol in his car. That was just a wise precautionary measure living in Zone 6.

A few days later Duke went to the pawn shop. You could be in and out of there with a weapon in no time. He got me a .380 and a box of bullets. This thing ended up being the most bullshit gun of all time. You could run up on someone and pull the trigger from point-blank range and still miss.

Of course I didn't know that when my brother handed it to me. I had never fired a gun.

That night I took a walk to nearby Glen Emerald Park. I pointed my new pistol to the sky and pulled the trigger until the clip was empty.

Pow! Pow! Pow! Pow! Pow! Pow!

Getting robbed was a turning point. Instead of making me retreat into my shell out of fear, it had the opposite effect. I became superaggressive. I knew when I shot my gun in the air that night that no one was going to take anything from me again. I would straighten out my business and everyone was going to know that if you fucked with me, there would be repercussions.

V

TEXACO

When I was fifteen, Duke moved out to start basic training for the US Army. Football hadn't worked out. After he left, things got real bad at home.

My father had been deteriorating for years. It finally reached a breaking point. All he lived for was the bottle. He didn't have any hustle left. He'd still go out to con folks, but he was so fucked up, no one was falling for his shit anymore. He got to be so delusional that he'd even try to con me. He'd drink until he got sick, go to the VA hospital, come home, and do it all over again.

"I can't go square for nobody," I remember him saying.

Soon after Duke left my parents got into a fight. Not verbal. Physical. That was uncommon, so the image remains clear in my head: my father hitting my momma across the face with the end of the vacuum cleaner, her falling to the ground as he stood over her and spit in her face. I tried to jump in but my father grabbed me by my throat, snatched the gold necklace he had given me clean off my neck, and threw me out of the way. The police came and my father was taken away on charges of domestic violence.

Gucci wasn't a bad person. No one who knew him would say he was. Ask any of my cousins in Alabama and I bet you they'd all say he was their favorite uncle. He was fun to be around, always offering words of encouragement for anyone he came across. Underneath his demons was a kind spirit. A good heart.

I've heard my cousin Suge compare me and my father to Floyd Mayweather Jr. and his pops. Floyd Sr. was a boxer and every bit the showman his son is. He taught his son everything he knew. The defense. The shoulder roll. The stiff jab. With his daddy's skills Floyd Mayweather Jr. did what his father hadn't been able to: put all the pieces together and become the greatest boxer of his generation.

Suge likens that story to me and my daddy, but the truth is I'm *still* putting the pieces together. I just think my father was never cut out for the whole family thing. Gucci could be the life of the party but in a lot of ways the man was a loner. He may have just been better off in life by himself. I loved my father, as did my momma, but there was nothing we could do for him. He was too far gone. His addiction was stronger than he was and it was tearing apart our home.

My brother went AWOL from the AIT school and came back home after I told him about the incident. Duke and Gucci's relationship had been strained for years. My brother did not want him coming back to the house.

Soon after my father's arrest we moved to another set of apartments off Bouldercrest called Sun Valley. Like Mountain Park, Sun Valley was infested with drugs and our new apartment was perched at the top of Sun Valley, which just so happened to be the spot where niggas sold dope.

There was constant traffic, so the move accelerated my hustle.

The top of Sun Valley was a prime trap, but at first I found it hard to compete with the older hustlers who operated there. The only reason I managed to was that I lived where I did. I would wait for those guys to retire for the night, seizing my opportunity to get my sacks off.

OJ moved from Mountain Park to Sun Valley around the same time I did. OJ and I had been buddies since the days of picking up cans, but because he was three years younger than me we'd mostly ran with different crews since then. Despite our difference in age OJ had been out on the corner hustling as long as I'd been. And he was good at it. OJ was a small guy, but he was never afraid to fight when shit went down. I always respected that.

When OJ moved to Sun Valley he moved to the bottom end of the apartments, so he *really* wasn't allowed to trap at the top. So he'd either be at the bottom, where they sold the weed, or he was up on Bouldercrest by the Texaco gas station. A lot of the time I was up there with him. Me and OJ have rapped about the damn Texaco so many times, so let me set the scene.

The Texaco is a place of trade, a spot where people can go to the store to buy a beer and some Swishers, then get some dope on their way out. A lot of folks preferred to go up there to shop—especially those who weren't completely fucked-up Js. Functioning crackheads, if such a thing ever did exist. I'm talking about people with jobs and families, but they still smoked crack. They'd rather come to the Texaco than have their kids and neighbors see them buy dope in the apartments.

The gas station is positioned on a busy five-way intersection. Custer Avenue connects with Bouldercrest. Bouldercrest connects with Fayetteville and Flat Shoals. Flat Shoals connects with Brannen Road. There's always traffic and there are two MARTA buses that stop there. The 32 Bouldercrest and the 34 Gresham. Years later OJ founded his rap label, 32 Entertainment, named after that bus stop.

We would post up, acting like we were waiting to catch the bus. When the 32 pulled up we'd tell the driver we were waiting for the 34, and when the 34 pulled up we'd say we were waiting for the 32. We'd be there for hours on end.

The Texaco was run by an Asian couple, Mr. and Mrs. Kim. Mr. Kim knew what was going on and for a while he was on our ass. He'd come outside and tell us to get away from the store and threaten to call the police. We'd leave for a couple of hours and come back. Sometimes we'd just tell him to step off. Eventually he gave up on trying to keep us out of there. We weren't going anywhere. I always wonder if Mr. and Mrs. Kim know how infamous their little gas station is.

> On Bouldercrest I'm sellin' dope at Texaco
> And Mr. Kim keep sayin' "Get 'way from sto!"
> No, I can't get 'way from sto, I got so much blow, it gotta go
> —"I'm a Star" (2008)

It wasn't some glamorous New Jack City type of shit. Countless nights I stood in the pouring rain, making plays, cold as hell, blowing into my hands to try to keep warm. It was the trenches.

A whole bunch of serious fights and shootouts went down at the Texaco too. It was the fall of 1997 when Javon got beat damn near to death outside the Texaco. Javon was OJ's best friend and a homeboy of mine. He got stomped out—fucked up really, really bad.

I felt terrible when I found out what had happened to Javon at the gas station. And I was concerned. Because I knew those niggas hadn't been out there looking for him. They'd come up looking for me.

Javon had been a casualty in an ongoing beef me and my boys had with a crew who called themselves the East Shoals Boys. The East Shoals Boys were from the other side of town, Decatur. Like the kids I'd gone to school with in Ellenwood, they weren't exactly well off, but they came from more nurturing environments than the crime-ridden projects I'd come up in. But they lived in the same school zone and attended McNair, which is where the Sun Valley Boys and the East Shoals Boys first butted heads.

On the last day of school my junior year—the spring of '97— a bunch of seniors had a huge food fight in the cafeteria. I'm sitting there and a whole bunch of shit got splattered all over me.

Immediately I stood up and walked over to the perpetrators. It was the baseball team. I slapped the shit out of one of them. Everyone, especially the one I slapped, was shocked. This was a senior *and* a jock and here was a junior slapping him silly in front of the whole cafeteria. He was so shook that he didn't do a damn thing about it.

Days later me and my buddies ran into the baseball team at a girl's graduation party in Decatur. There were maybe eight of us, but there were probably sixty of these dudes from that neighborhood. The minute they saw us, it was a problem.

Shit, we're about to get crushed.

They started grabbing baseball bats and the steering-wheel clubs from their cars and things were looking bad. They surrounded us and punked us out, but somehow we were able to get into our cars and get out of there without punches thrown. All in all a light confrontation.

But these dudes were still pissed and now it wasn't just the baseball team. After the confrontation at the party, that whole neighborhood took up those boys' cause, feeling like we had come in and disrespected their turf.

The school year was over, but throughout the summer I was hearing these guys were after me. When I started my senior year that fall, there were niggas roaming the halls looking for me. These weren't even guys who went to McNair. These were grown men from that hood.

After I heard what happened to Javon I knew I had to take action. Problem was I didn't have a lot of friends who were still at McNair. Save for OJ, all my friends were older than me. All the Sun Valley Boys had either graduated or dropped out. I was on my own at school.

"You need to come to school with me tomorrow," I told my buddy BP back at the apartments. "I can't show up there alone."

The next morning me and my crew boarded the school bus. Most of them had no business being on the bus, but the driver gave a nod of approval as we stepped on.

"Y'all better win," she told us. Even the bus driver had heard about what happened to Javon. She knew what time it was.

BP was fired up that morning. There was only one reason this nigga was headed back to his alma mater and that was to whoop some ass.

"Hey!" he screamed to the rest of the kids on the school bus. "Y'all are gonna help us fight or else we're gonna beat your fucking asses too when we get back to the apartments."

We had rallied up a crew of fifteen by the time we got to the school and there were around the same number of East Shoals Boys there waiting for us. BP didn't waste any time getting to it. He walked right up to one of them and knocked him out cold. It was on and poppin' from there. We fought for a long-ass time, beating the shit out of these dudes with chairs and all sorts of stuff lying around.

Satisfied with the beating we'd put on them, we took off running up Bouldercrest back to the apartments. We cheered as the police and ambulances zoomed past. We hid out the rest of the day at my buddy Dontae's and waited for things to die down.

VI

LAFLARE

I graduated from McNair in the spring of 1998 with a 3.0 GPA and a HOPE scholarship to Georgia Perimeter College. But I was doing pretty well for myself in the streets, so going back to school was the last thing on my mind. So I didn't go. I think they call that a gap year.

After I sat out the first two semesters, my momma gave me three options: go to school, get a job, or move out of her house. Since school was never difficult for me, enrolling at Georgia Perimeter seemed like the easiest option to keep her off my back.

I was an outsider at Georgia Perimeter. Whenever I did show up it was for the sole purpose of showing out. I had me a box Chevy with rims at the time and I'd pull up and hang out in the parking lot and try to talk to the coeds. I'd see my old classmates from McNair and how they were going through the whole college transition, trying to get their lives together. And there I was, pulling up in a nice car, with jewelry on my neck and dope-man Nike Air Maxes on my feet. I was flashy as hell. I liked shining on people. I was above it all.

That was pretty much the extent of my college experience. I don't have stories of frat parties or tailgating or whatever it is they do there. I was enrolled in some computer programming classes but I could count on both hands the number of times I showed up to class. When I first enrolled I worked the school out of like eighteen hundred dollars for textbooks. I took every dollar of that money and put it towards getting myself a bigger bomb. That's how serious I was about my studies.

My schooling would officially come to an end after I got busted at the Texaco. It was April 2001, my second semester at Georgia Perimeter.

Apparently an undercover cop had been watching me for a few days, and he found the bushes where I was keeping my stash at, a stash of about ninety bags of crack. I was in the gas station when he walked up and flashed his badge.

"Let me see your ID."

Knowing it would buy me time, I pulled out my driver's license and handed it over. The moment he took his eyes off me to inspect it, I was out the door.

I bolted through the backyard of a house on Custer into the woods, ending up in Glen Emerald Park. I blew past the tennis courts, leaping from the top basketball court to the bottom one. When I landed my legs gave out, all wobbly; I was like a boxer who took a shot on the chin. My mind was responding but my body was not. I collapsed on the court, knowing the cops were on my tail.

"I'm down! I'm down!" I screamed out.

My surrender didn't help my cause. Those cops beat the fucking shit out of me. I hadn't caught my breath from running when I was tossed in the back of the cruiser. I threw up all over the seats.

My face was swollen from the beating, so instead of taking me to the police station, where they'd have to take a mugshot, they took me to Grady Hospital. Afterward I was brought to DeKalb County Jail, where I was booked and told I was allowed one phone call. I called my momma.

"Momma, I'm locked up."

"For what?"

"They're saying 'criminal possession of a controlled substance,'" I said, doing my best to play dumb. "I was just standing at the bus stop, waiting to go for a job interview."

But the days of fooling my momma were up. Vicky Davis didn't play around about no drug shit. After I posted bail, she took my key to the house and told me I was no longer welcome at home.

•

When I went in front of the judge a few months later, I took a plea deal as part of Georgia's First Offenders Act. If I accepted the plea and completed a probation period, I could have this first felony struck from my record. But if I got caught "in any trouble" again, the deal was off the table, and the judge could resentence me.

"I'm giving you ninety days in county jail, Mr. Davis," he told me. "But do you understand that if I see you here again, I can sentence you up to thirty years in prison behind this?"

I heard him loud and clear, but I couldn't drop hustling cold turkey. I'd had nearly forty thousand dollars saved up at the time of my arrest, but I now had lawyer fees and had gotten my own apartment after my momma kicked me out the house. I needed to be making money.

Since I was still technically enrolled at Georgia Perimeter, my lawyer was able to convince the judge to suspend my ninety-day sentence until after the following school year, which was about to start up. So just like that I was out and it wasn't long before I was back to dibbling and dabbling in Sun Valley and the Texaco.

It might sound like the judge's warnings went in one ear and out the other, but that wasn't the case. I'd absorbed what he told me. Those words carried weight. I was back in the streets, yes, but for the first time in my life I was thinking about what I could do to get myself out of this shit. My decision to pursue music was heavily influenced by my arrest at the Texaco.

•

I'd long had a passion for music, ever since Duke and I were in Bessemer listening to his boom box. Even after we moved to Georgia, Duke was the guy who was putting everyone onto the new shit of the nineties, from 2Pac and Kilo Ali to Spice 1 and Poison Clan. He was tuned in, always on the cutting edge when it came to rap. And I absorbed it all. My whole childhood I was running circles around everyone my age. It was like how I learned to read before my peers. Whenever a new artist or song blew up and everyone in school was talking about it, it was old news to me. My brother had been put me onto it.

As much as I was into rap, the idea of becoming a rapper always seemed lame to me. The rappers I knew—classmates who used to perform at the McNair talent shows—were all broke. There was no way I was going to be the nigga with a backpack riding the MARTA bus with a CD player and headphones, trying to get people to listen to my music. To me that was panhandling. I didn't give a fuck if that's what it took to make it in the music business. It wasn't going to be something I did.

What *was* appealing to me was being the money man behind a rapper. I'd been heavy into Master P throughout high school. P was the consummate rap entrepreneur. No Limit was putting out albums every other day back then and I bought all of them just off the strength of P's cosign. I would have never bought a Fiend or Mac or Mia X album, but I listened to all of the No Limit albums to hear what P was saying.

Even before Master P, I always gravitated toward the CEO, the person in charge. As a little boy in Alabama, I liked Eazy-E more than Ice Cube. I thought Tony Draper was cooler than 8Ball or MJG. I wanted to be more like J. Prince than Scarface. Later on when Cash Money started blowing up, I knew right away that Baby and Mannie Fresh were my favorites. The Big Tymers fucked me up for real. I liked the shit they were talking about.

I had a friend whose younger brother decided he wanted to rap. He was fourteen and his moniker was Lil' Buddy. I saw potential in this kid and thought he could become a Kris Kross or Lil' Bow Wow type. And I could be the money man pulling the strings. I decided to give it a shot.

This same friend told me he knew of a producer whom I could buy some beats from to get my artist off the ground. So one day in 2001 he took me to a house in suburban Decatur, where I met a twenty-three-year-old beatmaker by the name of Zaytoven.

Zaytoven was new to Georgia. He'd grown up in the Bay Area, and following his father's retirement from the army, his family relocated to the South. Zay stuck around to finish high school in San Francisco but eventually joined his folks when he couldn't keep up with the cost of living out there.

When he got here he enrolled in barber college, which was where he'd met my friend. Zay was a good barber but a way better musician. He had a natural ear, having grown up playing piano and organ in church. With that foundation he'd become a hell of a producer.

Today Zay's sound is synonymous with the music coming out of Atlanta, but at the time that wasn't the case. His beats were superinfluenced by his roots in the Bay. He'd come up studying producers like DJ Quik and making beats for guys like E-40 and Messy Marv while he was still in high school.

He was the oldest in a family of four children and I sensed he was the spoiled favorite. His parents had converted the entire basement of their new home into a recording studio for him to pursue his craft. I didn't know what made a good studio or a bad one, but I could tell this setup had cost some money. It looked legit.

Zay and I could not have been more different. This was a guy who went to church every Sunday. He didn't drink, smoke, or curse. He had nothing to do with the type of things I had going in the streets. He came from a religious military family and his folks had kept him on the straight and narrow.

Despite our differences on paper, we clicked off the dribble. I was feeling his beats and I ended up buying a batch of 'em from him for a thousand dollars. With beats in hand I was ready to get to work with Lil' Buddy. But before I could do that, I had to report to DeKalb County to serve out my ninety-day sentence.

•

I get how for someone on the outside looking in, jail is an interesting place. Fortunately, for most people it's a world they'll never see. But the truth is that most of the time jail is just super boring. A whole lot of doing nothing. And when it's not boring, usually something bad is happening. Something that ain't really worth talking about.

Because it was my first offense, I was designated a trustee, which meant I'd only have to serve sixty-seven of the ninety days. I worked in the cafeteria and I talked a big game in there, telling the inmates I had my own record label and getting them to think I was established in the rap game. The truth was I hadn't done a damn thing.

The sixty-seven days flew by. When I came home it was time to back up all the talking I'd been doing. But I had to go back to the drawing board. My plans with the kid hadn't worked out. I'd only been gone two months, but that was long enough for a teenager to get distracted, decide he didn't want to be a rapper anymore, and move on to something else.

Now I was at square one and out of the thousand dollars I'd spent on Zay's beats.

I linked back up with Zay after my stint in the county. He suggested *I* start rapping and put the music mogul stuff on hold. Zay had seen me rap because I'd been writing the lyrics for Lil' Buddy and then telling him how to deliver them, giving him the flows. Zay thought I had talent. I wasn't so sure.

Not only did I have the stigma that rappers were all broke and lame, but I had long ago convinced myself that people would never take me seriously if I started up rapping.

It wasn't that I'd never rapped before. Far from it. Even before my brother put me onto his music, I had an interest in poetry and the process of putting words together in creative ways. I can't remember what I wrote but there was a day in first grade the teacher had our class make cards for Mother's Day. Everyone else's was on some "Roses are red, violets are blue . . ." shit, but I deliberated over that card until I could come up with something that didn't just rhyme but captured how I felt about my momma. It caught my teacher by surprise.

"Wow, Radric," she said. "This is how you really feel."

I colored the card and brought it home, excited to give it to my momma over the weekend. I sure as hell wasn't thinking about a rap career, but I did know this was something I was good at. Better than my peers.

After we moved to Georgia I'd spent a lot of time free-styling with my buddies in Sun Valley. Me and OJ would hang outside the apartments and take turns rapping while the other made a beat on the big green power generator. Me and my other friends—BP, C-Note, Dontae, Jughead, Gusto, and Joe—even had our own little rap crew. We called ourselves Home Grown. I always thought I was the best out of all of them. The thing was, whenever we would record our little ciphers on BP's cassette player, I hated how my voice sounded on playback.

I sounded different from my friends. My voice was that of someone from Alabama, not from Atlanta. Not only did I sound so country, but I'd always had something of a speech impediment, like my father had. I'd gotten teased for that in school after we moved to Atlanta and it was another factor that turned me off to the idea of becoming a rapper.

But something kept me coming back to Zay's basement,

and the more time I spent down there the more comfortable I became. I was playing around with my voice, my cadence, and my diction and after a while all those reservations I'd had slowly started to fade away.

I was listening to a lot of Project Pat then. I was twenty years old, coming into my own, and while I was out there doing what I was doing—trappin' out of cars with OJ and standing on the corner hustling—Project Pat was the soundtrack. I had his debut album from '99, *Ghetty Green*, on repeat. When a girl hopped in my car, that's what she was going to hear.

I'd always been a big fan of Memphis rappers. Guys like 8Ball and MJG, Kingpin Skinny Pimp, Tommy Wright III, Playa Fly, and Triple Six Mafia. But Pat was my favorite. Still is. He was talking that street shit and I just knew he was telling the truth.

I knew that life, and I could tell if a rapper was playing Scarface. I had an ear for that. I knew Project Pat did the shit he was rapping about. Can't nobody tell me different. I knew C-Murder did what he said. I knew Soulja Slim did what he said. I knew BG did what he said. Their music was real and it motivated me. My music had to be the same way.

P and Baby were my idols, but I couldn't be rapping about Bentleys and Ferraris because I wasn't living that life. The cars I was around were Regals and Cutlass Supremes. I couldn't be rapping about shutting down the clubs because I wasn't in the clubs. I was in the trap house. I was on the corner. I wanted my music to inspire niggas to get money and come up out of that shit, but at the same time I wanted to let them know I was one of them. I couldn't leave them out.

Soon I found myself at Zay's nearly every day. There wasn't a plan. We were just two young men trying to find ourselves, in music and in life. We didn't know the fun we were having would give birth to a whole genre and inspire a generation of artists after us.

Trap music. To some it's the subject matter. Stories of serving fiends through burglar bars. To others it's a style of beatmaking. Shit, today there's a whole audience of white kids who think trap music is about popping molly and going to a rave.

In a way it's all those things. But when I think about trap music I think about those early days in Zay's basement. When I would go over early in the morning after a night spent juugin' in my neighborhood. When Zay would mix our songs and he didn't even know how to mix. The whole process was crude and unrefined. What we were making wasn't radio-ready and definitely not destined for the charts.

When I think about trap I think about something raw. Something that hasn't been diluted. Something with no polish on it. Music that sounds as grimy as the world that it came out of.

•

Eventually I decided to put together my first body of work. I bought more beats from Zay and another producer I'd met named Albert Allen. Al had been the keyboard player for the nineties R & B group Silk and he knew a lot more than Zay or I about the music game. He helped me put together the collection of songs that would make up my first underground release. But first I needed a rap name.

People had always called me Lil' Gucci or Gucci's son, so it seemed like a good fit to take on my father's moniker. As for the release, I titled it *Str8 Drop Records Presents: Gucci Mane LaFlare*.

Str8 Drop was a crew I'd formed with my partner Whoa. It

wasn't a label as much as a group of niggas from my hood who were rapping. OJ was a part of this crew.

Al put me onto a place in the city that printed me a thousand CDs, posters, and postcards for *Gucci Mane LaFlare* and I hit the streets of East Atlanta hard with it. I was already a hell of a salesman and I worked my music into my day-to-day hustle, selling niggas a package deal for a dime of smoke and a CD. I would front copies to my homeboys and let them keep a couple of dollars for every CD they sold. It wasn't long after I printed up those first thousand CDs that I was almost out of stock.

At that point I arrived at a crossroads. Was I going to re-up on *Gucci Mane LaFlare* and try to move another thousand copies or was I going to figure out something else? My next move would be a pivotal one, one of the smartest decisions I made in my early music career.

I brought the last of my CDs, posters, and postcards to the bootleggers on the Westside of Atlanta by the Oakland City train station. I explained I was an up-and-coming artist out of the Eastside and that I was trying to get exposure for my music outside of my neighborhood.

"I need you guys to sell the hell out of this CD," I told them. "Whatever money that you get from it, it's yours."

"You sure?" they asked.

I assured them I was. To sweeten the deal, they printed me a few thousand duplicate copies of *Gucci Mane LaFlare* and posters for free, which I sold for two or three dollars a pop—all profit. More important, though, my music was now being pushed all throughout the state of Georgia.

VII

THE ZONE 6 CLIQUE

One day I was putting up my posters outside of Jazzy T's, a strip club on Columbia Drive on the Eastside, when I was approached by a dude who introduced himself to me as Red. Like me, Red was a rapper from East Atlanta and he knew my music. He'd heard my album and admired my hustle. We chopped it up, exchanged numbers, and agreed to meet up and work on music together.

Red and I became fast friends. We soon formed a group we named the Zone 6 Clique. The cornerstone of the Zone 6 Clique was a pledge to be self-sufficient, independent artists. We took pride in the fact that we were hustlers first and foremost. We had money and didn't need to sign to some label and get jerked over. This was a self-financed operation. Using profit from our dealings in the streets, we would fund and promote our own projects. But rapping wasn't yet my priority.

My whole crew from Sun Valley was made up of hustlers,

but Red and the rest of the Zone 6 Clique were on another level. Nearly everyone in the group was older than me. My game was petty compared to the shit they were up to. I was still picking up slabs of dope. They were getting powder by the kilo and cooking it up in trap houses. I was still a neighborhood corner hustler, slinging sacks. They were taking statewide trips, moving serious weight.

More than hustlers, they were robbers who targeted hustlers. They were robbing niggas for their stash and hitting big-time licks. They wouldn't think twice about taking someone's money on consignment—we're talking up to a hundred thousand dollars—and just saying "Fuck it" and driving off with no intention of paying anyone back. They didn't give a fuck about the consequences of pulling moves like that. They were more than willing to deal with them. Their whole attitude was bring it on.

It wasn't long before I was doing the same shit. Finessing people out of their money came naturally. It was in my genes. I knew whom I could short and whom I had to give extra to. I knew whom I could give some bullshit to and tell them it was good. I could sense if someone was weak or scared. I could feel it and use it to my advantage. I worked every move I could.

Hit a lick for 'bout 50 stacks
Niggaz trippin' talkin' 'bout Gucci bring the money back

I rapped that line in a song called "Lawnmower Man." It's a line that got me notoriety in my hood. Because it was true. Niggas couldn't believe I had the balls to talk about that incident on a track and it fortified my reputation as a rapper and a robber.

I started breaking into houses too. Not looking for TVs or

jewelry or anything like that. I was after money and drugs exclusively. I'd target those whom I'd previously shopped with, and after gaining their trust I'd hide out and wait for them to leave their stash house before breaking in. If I couldn't find it, I'd just sit in the house and wait for their return. Then I'd make them give it up. I quickly adopted the attitude of my new crew.

I accumulated enemies fast. My prey was my own hood. Even my closest friends from Sun Valley started distancing themselves after I aligned myself with the Zone 6 Clique, and those were not some soft niggas. They were superstreet too but they didn't condone robbing and tricking people out of their work. I'd bring my new crew around and they'd be looking at my buddies from Sun Valley like they were a steak. I kept them off them but that was only because I was targeting them for myself. At one point I even ended up taking BP's stash, and he was one of my best friends. That only alienated me from those guys even more. I'd become a slimy dude. My appetite had become insatiable.

In keeping up with my new partners I expanded my hustle beyond East Atlanta. I started going to cities, towns, and trailer park communities all over Georgia: Savannah, Milledgeville, Augusta, Sandersville, LaGrange, Brunswick, Thomson.

I also started taking regular trips to my home state of Alabama. I made that two-hour drive so many times. Sometimes twice in the same day because I'd moved the pack so quickly.

I didn't care for being back in Alabama. Ever since I'd gotten a taste of city life in Atlanta the country bored the hell out of me. Sitting around a fire, eating pig's feet, drinking, and shooting the breeze was not my idea of a good time. Everything in Alabama moved too slow. Everything, that is, except the money. The place was a damn gold mine.

•

Like Atlanta, the demand for drugs in Alabama was high, but unlike in the city there was a limited supply. For me that meant less competition and higher margins. The street value of everything was almost double what I'd make in Atlanta. So when I would show up in Birmingham with a couple of pounds of weed and half a ki of dope in tow, it was like Nino Brown was in town. I was bringing city ambition to these rural towns. A lot of these country-ass niggas had never seen anything like it.

My cousins in Bessemer trapped, so I made a good chunk of change in Alabama just off serving them. This was easy money but it brought problems. Inevitably my Alabama family discovered what I was up to. I was staying with my cousin Suge when my aunt Jean found the four pounds of weed I'd brought with me.

"Whose is this?!" she screamed. "What are you bringing into my house?!"

"Oh, Auntie, you know I like to smoke sometimes," I told her. I didn't miss a beat.

"Smoke?! You mean to tell me all of this is for you to smoke?!"

I can't imagine my auntie really believed that, but Suge and I managed to convince her not to flush it down the toilet. We eventually pinned it on my other cousin Trey, who agreed to take responsibility for it if I broke him off a little something later.

The stash was saved but not without consequence. My auntie knew what I was doing, which meant the rest of my aunties knew, which meant my uncles knew, which meant my momma knew. I'd once been the baby of the family. Now I was the black sheep. I started feeling like everyone dreaded my presence when

I'd come to Alabama. My aunties blamed me for what their kids were getting into. At the same time I had my cousins—all of whom were older—calling my phone when I'm in Atlanta, telling me it's dry down there and their pockets were hurting and I needed to come back and give them some work. It was a fucked-up dynamic.

My reputation in the family only got worse after Suge got arrested while he was runnin' with me. Just the night before Red and I had gotten into town. We caught up with Suge and his homeboy at this little trap house they had going in Jonesboro, on the side of Bessemer opposite from where Suge stayed at. There was a lot of action at this spot, but it was also a risky move because this was not Suge's neighborhood. The guys who claimed the area weren't keen on us out-of-towners showing up with better product at better prices. But I didn't give a fuck what they were or weren't keen on. So we trapped out of that house all night, making plays and smoking blunts until business dwindled down and we called it a night.

Hours later I awoke to the smell of smoke. The roof of the small shotgun house was in flames. Someone had thrown a firebomb. Our presence wasn't appreciated. I ran outside to find Red holding a hose, trying to extinguish the fire. But the hose couldn't reach the roof. I ran inside to grab the stash while Suge scrambled together our munition. We ran outside to load up the truck, knowing we had to split. Red kept at it with the hose. For a minute it seemed he was actually going to put it out, but once it spread to the insulation it was over with. We heard sirens and it was time to go. We took off, passing the fire trucks, and headed back to Suge's side of town, where we got a room at a motel to hide out and debrief.

Red wanted to return to Atlanta immediately and he had the right idea. This was a tiny community. Word traveled fast; people were going to hear about this. But I told him to head back solo because I didn't want to hang Suge and his buddy out to dry. After all, none of this would've happened if it wasn't for us showing up, and if I'd gotten my cousin into some sort of trouble, I needed to be there to get him out of it.

I stayed in Alabama for a few more days to see how everything played out. In the meantime I worked the remainder of the pack out of the motel. At some point I left to get something to eat. When I got back the stash was gone. I immediately suspected foul play. My instincts told me it was an inside job and that one of the housekeepers had robbed me. I called Suge and he showed up and got into it with the motel staff, demanding to see the security tapes. The motel called the law. Before I knew it the police were on the scene and Suge was in handcuffs. I made a run for it, hopping into Suge's car, fleeing for safety.

Damn.

I'd gotten my cousin arrested and his buddy's house burned down. And my family heard all about it. Even my brother was turned off by the trouble I was bringing around. He told my cousins they shouldn't mess with me anymore.

It hurt to see my family turn their backs on me but not enough to change anything. I was relentless. I had a girl in Birmingham and I started to operate out of her spot. She stayed in the middle of the projects and was popular there, so she set me up with many of my customers. One of them was her best friend, Amy. Amy sold weed, and whenever I'd come into town I'd serve her a QP (quarter pound). Amy had a boyfriend named Bunny. And Bunny was the first person to introduce me to lean.

For the uninitiated, lean is a drink made from mixing prescription cough syrup and soda. It was made popular in the nineties by DJ Screw, the Houston DJ who created Chopped and Screwed music. It's best known for being made with Sprite, but you can use anything for the soda. Mountain Dew. Kool-Aid. Crush. Some people add Jolly Ranchers or Skittles. Whatever. The part that matters is the pharmaceutical ingredient. Codeine and promethazine. That's the shit that puts you in another zone.

Bunny was a hustler too, and for a nigga from the sticks he moved a lot of weight. He didn't sell weed, which was why I would serve Amy, but he had them bricks. The four of us would hang when I was in town, on some double-date shit. Bunny didn't smoke but he did drink lean. And one night he offered me some.

"Gucci, I got some grit if you want it."

That's what they call it in Alabama. Grit. They don't call it lean. They call it grit because it's thick like grits and they drink it straight, like a shot. They don't put it in soda like how they do in Houston.

I didn't know the first thing about grit or lean or whatever this was, but I took Bunny up on his offer. Up to this point weed was the heaviest drug I'd used. But since I started running with the Zone 6 Clique, I'd been around them snorting powder, popping X pills, and lacing their weed with all types of junk. I figured this grit stuff couldn't hurt.

Amy poured the red syrup into a spoon and spread it inside the blunt she was rolling. Me and the two girls smoked the blunt while Bunny sipped his grit, and then we passed around the bottle, each of us taking a couple of swigs.

Everything was cool and after a while at Bunny's we decided to go to the Waffle House to get something to eat. That's where things get fuzzy. All I remember is that by the time we got up to leave, I was so out of it that I couldn't stand up out of my chair. I was stuck to it. I couldn't tell you how I made it out of there.

The lean had messed me up, but it wasn't until a few days later that I fully felt the effects of the drug. Out of nowhere, it seemed, I was totally out of my mind. It was like I couldn't control my thoughts. I found myself doing irrational shit I would never do normally, like giving people stupid deals on dope. I was thrown off, but I didn't yet make the connection to the lean.

Maybe I've been smoking too much.

Maybe someone put something in my drink at the Waffle House and tried to poison me.

I was still tripping when I got back to Atlanta a few days later and my symptoms had gotten worse than selling people dope on the cheap. My behavior was fucked up. I wasn't talking right. My pupils had gone dark. I'd become extremely paranoid and had turned aggressive toward everyone I came across.

Word got around the hood that something was up with me. When I came across my brother in the streets, he knew right away something was seriously wrong. Duke grabbed me by the arm and we took a long walk home to my momma's.

There was something strange about that walk. It was dreamlike. It brought me back to when my brother and I used to walk to school together. When we were living in East Atlanta but still going to school by Ellenwood, at Cedar Grove. After we got off the bus we would have to walk almost two miles to get to school every day, rain, sleet, or snow.

My momma and Duke took me to the hospital, where I stayed for a couple of days until I started to feel like myself again. It's hard to describe this episode, or the similar ones that followed in the years to come, but I knew when it was over with. I felt normal again.

None of the doctors had answers. I hadn't told them I'd been drinking straight cough syrup because that wasn't something people did in Atlanta, and honestly it hadn't occurred to me that that's what could have caused this shit. Nobody else who drank the grit that night had tripped out. I was really convinced someone had slipped something into my drink, because that was actually something that was going on then. Folks getting drugged and then losing their minds out of nowhere.

Years later, when things were completely out of control and it was obvious what I was doing to myself, a doctor told me I had to cut it out with the lean.

"Listen, you cannot drink this stuff anymore. It's causing a chemical imbalance in your body," he explained. "This drug is just not for you."

By that point I was drinking it first thing in the morning and last thing at night to fall asleep. My stomach had ballooned to the size of a watermelon. I looked pregnant. Even then I wasn't ready to hear that. I couldn't accept that this drug had become my kryptonite.

After that first incident I refrained from drinking lean for a while. It wasn't that I was worried I would trip out again. It just hadn't been a feeling I particularly enjoyed, being glued to my seat at the Waffle House. Lean wasn't even something widely available in Atlanta then. It was a Houston thing.

It wasn't until I met Doo Dirty that I started to get hooked. Doo Dirty was Red's homeboy from Savannah, and he was the big man down there.

Savannah has a totally different culture from Atlanta. People in Savannah talk different, they dress different. The way folks move there mirrors Florida more than it does Atlanta, being that it's only two hours away from Jacksonville and not far from Miami. It's a port city, so a lot of drugs from overseas come through. And drugs were Doo Dirty's specialty. He kept a lot of 'em around.

Doo Dirty put me onto pouring lean in a soda can, which I found to be a much different experience. It tasted good and I didn't react like when I drank it straight. I'd drank an ounce straight down the hatch that first night with Bunny, but now I was pouring an ounce or two in a two-liter of soda and sharing it among a crew. It tasted like candy to me and I loved the high. It relaxed me and alongside the weed put me in a zone I really enjoyed. As my body absorbed the codeine a wave of calm would wash over me. Not a care in the world.

I also thought it was cool that this was something people weren't doing in Atlanta. It was taboo. In Doo Dirty I found a plug with constant access. That gave me status.

He also turned me on to ecstasy. I had never fucked with pills before but Doo Dirty would drive up from Savannah in his old-school dump—a '73 Chevy with rims—and he'd have milk gallon jugs filled to the top with pills for us to sell. We started selling these pills and soon we were popping them. Long story short, soon enough I was regularly fucking with hard drugs.

But the Zone 6 Clique wasn't all drugs and stealing. As much as running with my new partners accelerated my hustle game, it made me step up my rap skills even more. These were street niggas but they also had talent and were serious when it came to their music. The Zone 6 Clique studio sessions were competitive. Everyone was coming hard and it brought something out of me I hadn't yet discovered. I'd felt good about the work I put in when I first started up with Zay, but now I was paying closer attention to my lyrics and delivery, approaching the craft of rapping in a more focused and disciplined way.

For Doo Dirty, the Zone 6 Clique was an opportunity to get involved in the rap game. For a minute he'd been telling us about this dude from Detroit. Big Meech. I had never heard of Meech or his Black Mafia Family crew, but Doo Dirty was saying this nigga was a serious hustler who was trying to make some legal money in the music business. He wanted to follow their lead. I remember thinking it was crazy to hear him singing the praises of this guy I'd never heard of because to me, Doo Dirty was the shit. He was the richest nigga I knew.

And so just like Meech with BMF Records, Doo Dirty became the CEO of the Zone 6 Clique Music Group, pumping big money into promoting the group. We'd all go out and hit the clubs and D had us in there looking like established artists. We now had Z6C chains, Z6C letterman jackets, and with D's financing we put together thirty thousand dollars to shoot a video for "Misery Loves Company," my first-ever music video. Look it up.

The footage is grainy but if you look closely you'll see I had a busted-up lip. Two days before the shoot I got jumped at Jazzy T's. I was in the bathroom taking a piss at the urinal when some nigga came up from behind and sucker-punched me. Next thing

I knew there were four of them, beating on me in the bathroom. Somehow I managed to escape and scramble out of the club. I took cover at a nearby motel until Red came and got me.

I later found out the attack was stemming from an incident that occurred a couple of weeks prior. A guy had bought like a hundred dollars' worth of smoke off me but overpaid me by more than a thousand dollars. He'd given me a bankroll with a bunch of fives and ones on top but as I kept counting I discovered hundreds underneath. When he tried calling me about the mistake, of course I ignored the calls. I never saw those guys again, nor could I say I would have remembered them.

Doo Dirty also put the money up for my first collaboration with a major artist. We were down in Florida for a celebrity basketball game and Juvenile was one of the featured guests. Juve was superhot at the time and I was a fan, so I walked up on him and introduced myself, asking if he'd be interested in doing a verse for one of my songs.

"Yeah I'll do a feature for you," he told me. "Seventy-five hundred."

I didn't have seventy-five hundred on me and neither did D, but I was good for it. So I called up Whoa, from my neighborhood crew Str8 Drop, and he told me he'd go half. He'd wire the money via Western Union and after I got back to Atlanta I'd pay him back $3,750. Done. We got the money wired to Juve's brother Corey and we were good to go. Corey had us meet them at their hotel, where the plan was to knock out the song in the makeshift recording studio on Juvenile's tour bus.

I was excited about this. I was twenty-three years old and I was about to get a guest verse from the hottest artist on the hottest record label, Cash Money Records. This could be big. But when I got on the bus Juve flipped the script. He said he wanted to make me a beat and he'd do a chorus for it.

"See I told my partner back in Atlanta that I was getting a verse, though," I told him.

Juve didn't budge.

"Look, I'm going to make you this beat and then I'll knock out the hook for it."

Flipping the script on niggas like this was my game. I wasn't going to get tricked out of a verse I'd paid for.

"Why would I want a beat from you?" I finally blurted out. "You're not Mannie Fresh."

The whole bus went silent after I said it. I could see Juvenile was pissed.

"What I am is a platinum-selling artist," he told me. "So I'm not doing a guest verse for *you*."

"A'ight, well then I don't want anything."

With that, Juve pointed me to the door.

"No disrespect, but you need to get off my bus then," he told me. "I'll get the money wired back to you."

Juve had taken a liking to my boys, so I was the only one asked to leave, which I did without any hoopla or words exchanged. While it may have seemed like I'd just gotten punked out I wasn't embarrassed in the least. I was proud of how I'd handled the situation. I'd told Whoa I was getting Str8 Drop a Juvenile verse and he'd put his money down for that. So I wasn't coming back to him with a beat and a hook. For me this was a business arrangement and I had to stand firm on what we'd agreed on.

I was waiting outside the bus for my buddies when Wacko and Young Buck, two well-known artists who were running with Juvenile at the time, hopped off the bus to smoke a blunt.

"Man, don't even worry about that shit back there," Wacko told me, passing me the blunt. "Juve be on his bullshit sometimes."

Doo Dirty got off the bus a couple of minutes later and tried to get me to patch things up. I didn't think there was anything to patch up. I had no problem with Juvenile. I'd just meant what I said. I wasn't interested in paying that much money for a Juvenile beat. I didn't even know the nigga made beats.

"Here's what we'll do," D told me. "Let the wire transfer go through, we'll get the beat and the hook, and when we get home I'll give you the money for it."

I knew if anyone was good for seventy-five hundred it was D, so I agreed and let them proceed with the song. After all I didn't have an issue with a Juvenile beat and hook if I wasn't the one paying for it. Wacko and Buck respected how I'd handled myself in there and invited me back on the bus, now that we were moving forward with the record. But I just waited outside until they finished.

"I don't need to get back on the bus," I told them. "Let's just do the song."

That song with Juvenile never ended up amounting to anything, but it was my first experience interacting with a major artist. Years later I saw Juvenile and we both pretended like it was our first time meeting. We swapped songs over at Patchwerk Studios in Atlanta. Everything went smoothly. I respected Juvenile. But I knew as soon as I saw him that he remembered that day. I didn't say anything about it because I didn't see a reason to bring up a negative experience that was in the past. But I could just tell he remembered.

I burnt the last of my bridges when I tricked Doo Dirty's

nephew out of thirty thousand dollars while I was down in Savannah. That was a dumb move, and a messed-up one too because D had always looked out for me.

Now I had these young boys from Savannah plotting to come to Atlanta and kill me. And they knew where I stayed. Even if I switched up spots, I worried someone would tip them off. I'd become such a menace in my hood there were a lot of people that wanted to see me get shot up.

So I left, retreating to Alabama, where I lay low for a couple of months, waiting for the beef to die down.

Some niggas tried to wet me up
Shot up my truck in East Atlanta
Want to set me up because I tricked this nigga in Savannah
They put some money on my head, I had to move to Alabama
　　　　　　　　　　　　　　　—"Frowny Face" (2008)

After a few months I decided to return to Atlanta. I couldn't take it. The place was too slow for me. I'd enrolled in the barbering program at Lawson State Community College in Birmingham but I only went to class once. I didn't want to cut hair. I wanted to get back to trapping and making music.

I tried to fly under the radar after I came back, lying low at Danielle's spot. Danielle was my on-and-off girlfriend from age twenty to twenty-five. She was a pretty girl who was as hood as I was. Very rough around the edges. She would help me bag up and stash my money for me. It wasn't love, but she knew me well and was an asset to the things I had going on then.

I was keeping a low profile because I didn't know if Doo

Dirty's nephew and his boys were still out looking for me. But one day I left the house to grab some Swishers from the gas station. When I drove up, guess who was standing outside: Red. He had a newborn baby in his arms and was talking to a girl I recognized. This was a girl who stayed in Augusta. We used to trap out of her trailer park there.

For a few minutes I sat in my car in the parking lot of a Popeye's, watching them. Seeing them interact with the baby, I realized Red had had a child with this girl while I was away.

Then I realized what they were up to. He was loading her down and fitting to put her on the road. The gas station was right off the expressway. Any minute now she was going to hop on the exit and start the two-hour drive to Augusta with birds in tow.

I had a laugh to myself, knowing I'd peeped the move. I wanted to get out of the car and go say what up, but I didn't know where Red and I stood anymore. He and I never had any fallout, but he was so tight with D and I'd put D in this terrible situation by robbing his nephew.

Why would I do that?

As I sat there watching them, thinking back on how everything had played out these last few months, an SUV pulled into the gas station and parked next to Red and his girl. Out stepped the big man of Savannah and CEO of Zone 6 Clique Records himself, Doo Dirty.

On pure instinct I hopped out of the car and headed toward them. I didn't know what was about to happen but I did know one thing: I was tired of hiding.

Before I reached them D and Red saw me coming and ran to meet me, hugging me, telling me how much they'd missed me.

"You know I paid off that bounty, right?" D asked me. "They were going to shoot up your momma's house so I paid it off."

I hadn't known that, and it fucked me up. Not only the idea of niggas putting bullets in my momma's crib but that despite everything, D was still looking out for me. Apparently he'd told my mother it was safe for me to come home, but she never relayed the message. She probably didn't know if it was a setup and likely felt I was better off in Alabama anyway.

The Zone 6 Clique was back in business. I'd missed Red and I'd missed Doo Dirty, and most of all I'd missed making music, which had been put on hold in my hiatus. I wasn't alone in that feeling. Red and D were ready to get to work as well. I left my car in the Popeye's parking lot and we piled into D's truck and headed to a house out in Clayton County that belonged to a producer I hadn't worked with before. His name was Shawty Redd.

Shawty Redd was working with Red on some stuff, and after they wrapped he played some beats and I liked his sound. They were as hard as Zay's but a totally different style. I also liked how quickly he could knock out instrumentals. He worked at my speed.

Shawty Redd and I exchanged numbers, agreeing to link back up to work on new music, which I was eager to get started on.

Before we left, Shawty Redd told me he wanted to introduce me to someone he'd been working with who was a fan of mine. His name was Young Jeezy. He had him on the phone.

Jeezy told me he fucked with this song "Muscles in My Hand" off *LaFlare* and that one of these days we should work together. Shawty Redd played me a few of this guy's songs earlier in the afternoon and to me, he sounded like a poor man's Trick Daddy.

Which was fine, no problem, I just wasn't paying him much mind.

Doo Dirty and Red dropped me back off at the Popeye's parking lot where I'd first seen them earlier in the day. Danielle was there waiting for me. She'd been worried sick. She'd seen my car parked there on her way home from work and had been calling my phone, which was dead. She didn't know if I was out creeping with another girl or if something had happened to me. She'd waited for hours.

Danielle really didn't know what to think when she saw me pull up with D and Red. But I told her what happened and that everything was going to return to normal. The bounty on my head had been paid off and the Zone 6 Clique had my back again. It was time to get things going.

VIII

GIFT AND CURSE

In the fall of 2003 a rap group from the Westside of Atlanta called Dem Franchize Boyz released a song called "White Tee." It blew up. These guys didn't do too much after that, but at the time "White Tee" was everywhere.

I liked "White Tee" but it was tame and kid-friendly, so me and a couple of the guys from Str8 Drop came up with "Black Tee." We put a sinister spin on it, rapping about robbing and selling drugs.

I rob in my black tee,
Hit licks in my black tee,
All in ya house lookin' for bricks in my black tee
I kill in my black tee
I steal in my black tee
I'm real so I gotta keep it trill in my black tee
                                        —"Black Tee" (2004)

"Black Tee" received attention from the jump, being that it was a crew out of the Eastside responding to a group from the Westside. But as the song started getting radio play, nobody knew a thing about the group behind it. I just happened to have the first verse on there and I plugged my name in it, so DJs started to credit it as my record.

And now here's "Black Tee," by Gucci Mane and the Black Tee Boys.

Ever the opportunist, I ran with that and started going to clubs promoting "Black Tee" as my song. For the first time my name was buzzing in Atlanta.

I started performing "Black Tee" at any bar, nightclub, or strip joint that would let me get on the mic. These were not paid performances. A lot of times I had to pay to perform. In the months that followed I built a following at the club Singles on Moreland Avenue, which was in walking distance from the Knights Inn we'd moved to with my father in '89. Singles was later renamed Libra Ballroom.

I performed at the Libra two to three nights a week on open mic nights. I would often record a song at Zay's, then test it out that night at the Libra. It gave me immediate and real feedback to my music. The Libra was notorious for shootouts, bar fights, and showin' out, but a lot of local talent got their start there. Yung LA, OJ da Juiceman, Yung Ralph, and Peewee Longway were a few of the artists I used to see there.

There was already friction between me and the Str8 Drop family. We'd lived so close to each other for so many years that petty rivalries and jealousies developed. So when I started running with "Black Tee" as my own song, the tension escalated to conflict. Str8 Drop and the Zone 6 Clique collided at the

Libra one night and that was the end of my affiliation with Str8 Drop. They later changed their name to Neva Again, a pledge to never again deal with me. I was done with the group by the time they decided to shoot a video for "Black Tee" and they had some other nigga with a bandana covering his face, rapping my verse.

Performing "Black Tee" one night at the Libra, I met Lil' Scrappy. Scrappy was still on the come-up—this was before "Money in the Bank"—but as an up-and-coming artist signed to Lil Jon, he was hot in the city. People definitely knew Lil' Scrappy.

Scrappy had a feud going on with Dem Franchize Boyz and told me he wanted to jump on a remix of "Black Tee." That was perfect for me because I needed to figure out how to keep rolling with this song now that I wasn't on good terms with the rest of the rappers on it. We set up a time to meet up later that week and do the remix.

A few days later Scrappy and I were at Patchwerk Studios doing the "Black Tee" remix. As we were finishing up I saw Bun B and Killer Mike leaving Patchwerk's other recording room. These were two rappers I had a lot of respect for. I was a longtime UGK fan and I liked Killer Mike's music too. I introduced myself.

When they asked about me I explained I was the guy from "Black Tee" and that I was here with Lil' Scrappy to do the remix.

Bun B and Killer Mike were both familiar with the song, and to my surprise Bun offered to hop on the remix for thirty-five hundred dollars.

"Give me a thousand dollars and I'll get on there too," Killer Mike added.

This was a hell of a deal. I was about to get Lil' Scrappy, Bun B, and Killer Mike on my song for forty-five hundred. For them to charge me such a cheap price I knew they must have seen my drive and respected my hustle. I hit up Doo Dirty and he immediately agreed to foot the bill for the features. We all headed back inside the studio, where Bun B and Killer Mike laid down their verses. While Bun was finishing his, I rang up Jody Breeze, another homegrown talent who was signed to renowned producer Jazze Pha's Sho' Nuff Records. He and I had gotten cool on a chance encounter at Atlanta's infamous strip club Magic City. I'd recently had him get on another song of mine for five hundred dollars and a zip of smoke. He said he'd pull up and get on "Black Tee" for free.

The "Black Tee" remix was finished and hard as hell. The next day I printed a few hundred copies to pass out to DJs and get it circulating through the city.

Two days later me and my boys were at Walter's, a clothing shop downtown, dropping off copies of the remix. While my buddies tried on gear I went next door to another store called What's Happenin' to leave a few CDs. While I was inside, a man approached me, introducing himself as Coach K.

Coach K managed Young Jeezy, and he had been looking for me to get us to collaborate. Apparently we'd kept missing each other at Shawty Redd's, where we'd both been working of late. I remembered then that Shawty Redd had put me on the phone with this dude. Turned out Jeezy was next door at Walter's, so we convened in the parking lot across the street.

Jeezy was from Macon, about an hour and a half south of Atlanta. He'd moved to the city some years back and was now running with Big Meech and BMF.

Remember when I said me and my boys had never heard of Meech or BMF back when Doo Dirty first told us about them? Well, by the time I met Jeezy everyone in the city knew those names. I swear it felt like it happened overnight. Things in Atlanta had been one way and then BMF happened.

These niggas were hitting all the hot spots—Club Chaos, Compound, the Velvet Room—and shutting shit down, pulling up in foreign sports cars, buying bottles of Cristal by the case and throwing around stupid money. Tens of thousands of dollars in a night like it was nothing. Nobody had ever seen that before. Meech and them invented making it rain. The BMF story isn't my story to tell, but man, it was something else. They were really putting on.

While I was aware of Meech I still wasn't familiar with Jeezy beyond our phone call at Shawty Redd's. But he seemed cool enough and I appreciated that he was fond of my music. We agreed to meet up the next day to see if we could get some songs going.

Before parting ways we swapped CDs. I handed him the "Black Tee" remix and he gave me his new mixtape, *Tha Streets Iz Watchin'*.

I popped it into the CD player of the truck as we pulled off and the shit was hard. As a group we decided it was a good idea to work with this guy. Two days later we were at Patchwerk.

But Jeezy and I weren't on the same page when we got in the studio. After we played a few beats and tossed some ideas around it seemed like we might not get anything off the ground. Jeezy was saying he wanted to make something real street and grimy, but I didn't care for any of the beats he was playing.

"Is it cool if I have my partner Zaytoven come through?" I finally asked. "His beats are really good."

With a green light I rang up Zay, who was cutting hair at the barbershop. I told him he needed to get down to Patchwerk ASAP and save this session.

Zay had given me a CD of beats recently and there was one on there I was stuck on. I'd first listened to it while heading out of town with the Z6C boys. We were riding to Daytona to get up with Daron "Southboy" Fordham, an ex–football player turned filmmaker. Daron was making a movie, *Confessions of a Thug*—it was like a hip-hop musical—and he wanted the Zone 6 Clique to make a cameo in it.

I'd come up with a hook for this beat in the car but hadn't found the chance to get to the studio with it. But the hook was stuck in my head.

Zay loaded the beat and let it play. As it did I kept humming my hook to Zay.

"Okay, forget about everything else you guys have been doing here," he said. "This is the song you need to do."

I'd never seen him so adamant and I trusted his instincts. Coach K agreed.

"Yeah, let's try it," he said.

I had been humming the melody of this hook more than singing it because I wasn't much of a singer. But Jeezy had a friend at the session named Lil' Will from Atlanta's legendary Dungeon Family, who could sing for real. So I wrote down the lyrics to the hook.

All these girls excited
Ooo ya know they like it
I'm so icy, so icy
Girl, don't try to fight it
All yo friends invited
I'm so icy, so icy

As soon as Lil' Will laid down the hook everybody in the studio was on board. Well, almost everyone. Jeezy still didn't like it. It wasn't the grimy street sound he was used to. It was melodic with a catchy hook.

"Let's just do some street shit," Jeezy insisted. "Something edgier."

Some kind of way Coach and Jeezy's crew persuaded him to do it. We did our verses and as soon as we finished copies were pressed. A few days later Jeezy asked if he could get on the "Black Tee" remix too, coming in right after Bun B's verse. I was all for it. We'd only known each other a few days but everything was coming together nicely.

Collectively we started pushing "So Icy" and the "Black Tee" remix heavy. Doo Dirty and even Meech, whom I still hadn't met, would be in the clubs tossing bands around to get the strippers and DJs on board with the songs. Before I knew it Hot 107.9 and V-103 had them on heavy rotation. My buzz in Atlanta blew the roof off. Suddenly everyone wanted a piece of Gucci Mane.

•

It wasn't long before labels came knocking. The first to offer me a deal was T.I.'s Grand Hustle. I had known Clay Evans, the vice president of the label, from before "Icy." He knew me from the open mic nights at the Libra and he'd taken an interest in my career. The first shows I ever got paid for were through Clay. He took me out to Chattanooga and small towns in Alabama and got me like five hundred dollars to perform, which was nothing, but I was so happy that I was actually getting paid to perform my music. I've still got love for Clay because of that. I even shouted him out on a song years later.

> *T.I. many times encouraged, told me face the game*
>   *with courage*
> *Clay gave me some great advice and still today I'm*
>   *thankful for it*
>
>   —"Worst Enemy" (2009)

Clay and Jason Geter, the other top dog at Grand Hustle, offered me a fifty-fifty partnership. They would foot the bill for producing and promoting my music and then we'd split the profits. But they weren't offering any money up front.

Clay wanted me to meet T.I. He brought me to the video shoot for Slim Thug's song "3 Kings" that T.I. and Bun B were featured on. T.I. was locked up in Fulton County for a probation violation on a drug conviction at the time, but he was in a work release program where he was allowed to record and conduct business during the daytime.

This was the old T.I., gold grill in his mouth and iced-out chains around his neck. He and I clicked and over the next few weeks were regularly in touch. But I ended up declining Grand Hustle's offer. They needed an answer and I needed more time to think things through. The success of "Black Tee" and "So Icy"

1

2

3

4

5

6

7

8

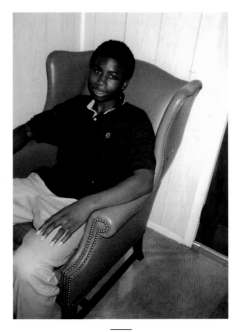

9

was happening so fast and even I wasn't sure of what I was looking for in a record deal. I think he ended up signing Young Dro instead.

But Grand Hustle wasn't the only one who wanted to sign me. I was hotter than fish grease. One night, while I was performing at a club, I met a member of another local rap group called the 404 Soldierz. He was a producer and wanted to get me on some of his beats.

Later that week I got a call asking if we could meet up, because there was someone he wanted me to meet. I pulled up to the parking lot of the West End Mall. That's when I met Jacob York.

Jacob was the son of Dwight York, also known as Malachi York, the founder of the infamous Nuwaubian Nation, a cult religious group that built a compound in Putnam County, Georgia. I'd heard of Malachi, who had recently pleaded guilty to 116 counts of child molestation, but I wasn't familiar with Jacob, who was telling me that he had been in the music industry for a long time. He said he had been instrumental in brokering the careers of the Notorious B.I.G., Lil' Kim, Cam'ron, Pastor Troy, and a bunch of other artists from the South. His reputation had earned him his nickname "the Chancellor." Most of this turned out to be true but at first I found it all hard to believe.

Jacob backed up his talk when he flew me to New York City to meet with the majors. He had us up at the W Hotel on Lexington Avenue and 49th Street. As soon as we checked in he told me he wanted me to meet Cam'ron, who was about to pull up to the hotel.

This was dope. Me and Zay were big fans of Cam'ron and

the whole Dipset movement. Cam wasn't just one of my favorite New York rappers, he was one of my favorite rappers period. Plus Jacob had shown me a photo of Cam's latest purchase—a royal-blue Lamborghini—so I was I excited to see both of them.

"He's really just riding around the hood in that Lambo by himself?" I asked Jacob.

"Well, this ain't exactly the hood, Gucci." Jacob laughed. "This is Manhattan, but yeah, he's coming by himself."

To my surprise Cam pulled up to the W in a Toyota Camry. At least the shit was new. He'd just bought it for his mother and was taking it out for a test drive. He wasn't decked out in some bright pink fur like I'd expected him to be either. He was dressed regular. Meanwhile I was wearing a North Carolina blue mink coat and my recently acquired forty-thousand-dollar "So Icy" chain.

We chopped it up and I liked Cam. He was humble and I could tell he had some street in him too. He was for real. He wished me luck on my trip to the labels and we parted ways.

Jacob and I did the rounds over the next two days and met with all the majors—Bruce Carbone at Universal, Kedar Massenburg at Motown, Craig Kallman at Atlantic, Lyor Cohen at Warner Bros. But I wasn't impressed with what they had to offer and frankly, none of them seemed all that impressed with me. My network inside the industry was minimal and I had barely traveled outside of Georgia. They all had the same script; they could put me in movies or get me on tour with so-and-so rapper. What I was interested in was money and being the head of my own label with their financial backing. I wasn't hearing that anyone wanted to give me that.

There was one person who did. Todd Moscowitz. Todd had just been named president of Asylum Records, the storied label founded by the legendary David Geffen. Asylum built its reputation on classic rock but had reinvented itself by specializing in hip-hop and R & B. Todd had signed a bunch of artists from Houston, a hotbed of talent at the time. So he, more than any of the other label heads, seemed to be genuinely excited about music coming out of the South.

But I didn't know what to make of this guy. Here was this white Jewish dude from New York City with a Mohawk basically telling me he wanted to write me a blank check. Somehow he got Lyor and Kevin Liles on board, and even the pioneering exec Chris Lighty was in the mix. Todd wanted me bad.

But his enthusiasm scared me off. I had trust issues from my dealings in the streets and I was coming from a group where our worst nightmare was getting fucked over in a deal. Todd telling me he'd give me whatever I wanted was just too brazen. So Jacob and I headed back to Atlanta without a deal. I didn't know what to make of these labels, but my trip to New York had opened my eyes, giving me a sense of my worth in the larger industry.

Jacob wasn't sold on doing a deal with the majors anymore either. He didn't feel they understood the southern rap scene and was concerned that I'd be mismanaged as an artist under a New York–based label. So when we got back to Atlanta, Jacob set up a meeting with a small, local independent label named Big Cat Recordings.

Big Cat was Marlon Rowe. This man was fat as hell, well over three hundred pounds. He was a friend of Jacob's from New York but was from Kingston, Jamaica, and had spent a good portion of his life in Fort Lauderdale. As funny-looking as this dude was, I quickly gathered he was no dummy and I sensed he'd been in the streets prior to the music game.

Cat was a street dude and a millionaire but he wasn't the type to tell you all about it. He flew under the radar. Reserved and quiet, but a very smart, savvy independent businessman.

Like Grand Hustle, Cat wanted to do a fifty-fifty partnership, except that he offered money up front to reimburse me for all I'd spent investing in my career to date, which was a lot.

Doo Dirty, Red, and the rest of the Zone 6 Clique weren't pleased with the idea of me signing with Big Cat. By no means were we broke, and the buzz from "So Icy" was getting bigger by the day. Why not just wait it out? But I saw things differently.

Unlike Doo Dirty, Cat had real experience putting out albums, and Big Cat Records was way more legit than Z6C. His other artists were bullshit but he had an office, studio, radio contacts, DJs in pocket, and a whole promotional street team. Plus Jacob would be involved and Jacob had a track record. I knew at this stage I was better positioned to make it if I partnered with these guys.

And that's what I did. As part of a joint venture with Big Cat, with distribution through Tommy Boy Records, I formed my own label, LaFlare Entertainment.

As all this was going on Def Jam decided they wanted "So Icy" for Jeezy's upcoming debut album. Jeezy was the shit at the time. He'd followed up *The Streets Iz Watchin'* mixtape with *Trap or Die*, a release that was the soundtrack of the city. He was ridin' with BMF, and they were running the show in

Atlanta. He had a solo deal with Def Jam and then a group deal with Boyz N Da Hood under Puff Daddy's Bad Boy Records.

But even with all that hype and industry backing, Jeezy didn't have a breakout song. "So Icy" was the first time a Jeezy song had gone into radio rotation. Jeezy had "Over Here" and don't get me wrong, that was definitely killing the clubs, but the radio wasn't playing him. That wasn't even out of the ordinary. That's how records break out of Atlanta, from the strip clubs up. Having my second single played across the country—that was out of the ordinary.

Def Jam offered me a hundred thousand dollars for the rights to "So Icy." Before that offer came in I'd finally met Meech, who wanted to get the song for himself and put his artist Bleu DaVinci on there. I requested some crazy amount from him and he passed. Even then Meech was cool about the situation and continued to promote the song in the clubs regardless. Meech and I were always cool. It wasn't until I declined Def Jam that things started to turn sour.

•

Jeezy and I were never friends, but during the rise of "So Icy" we would occasionally hit the clubs to perform the record. When I turned down Def Jam's offer, those joint performances stopped. Word was it was because Jeezy had a problem with me.

Jacob had known Jeezy for years, from when he was in south Georgia making crunk music as Lil' J. So he set up a meeting at Piccadilly's to squash whatever needed to get squashed.

I'd been hearing all this junk in the streets, but I still had no idea where the bad blood was coming from. It wasn't coming from me.

Right away it was clear nothing good was coming out of that meeting. The vibe was fucked. Honestly it caught me off guard. This guy had a *real* problem with me. It was no longer a business situation to sort out. It had become personal. Jacob was open to having the song included on both of our albums, but Def Jam wouldn't agree because my album with Big Cat was scheduled to come out first. Jeezy had already put the song on his *Trap or Die* mixtape and we weren't even tripping over that.

But he was pissed and couldn't even say why.

"He knows what he did," he mumbled, his eyes looking down at the table. That was all he said.

To his credit Jacob was able to convince Jeezy we should still shoot a video for "So Icy" and do a remix. It was no reconciliation but it would benefit both of us.

The plan was to pull Boo off the song, then Jeezy and I would record new verses for the remix. Jeezy did his and then stepped out to go to the bathroom or something. As I was recording mine Jeezy barged back into the studio.

"What the fuck?!" he shouted. "You got niggas out here trying to press me?!"

I exited the studio and found Black Magik, another rapper signed to Big Cat. Weapons had been drawn.

I wasn't sure if Magik had tried to rob Jeezy or chump him, but some sort of altercation had just taken place. Jeezy was fuming and understandably so, and he was thinking I'd set him up. But I had no idea what was going on. So I was pissed too. What the fuck was Magik doing coming up to my session, pulling shit that was going to fuck up my money? I was here working and now Magik was coming in and causing problems.

I got Magik to leave and Jeezy seemed to understand that I hadn't been involved. Still, he was furious. What could have been a final opportunity for us to find common ground became an opportunity for further conflict.

From there everything went downhill quick. I was working on finishing my album, but it seemed like half the city was beginning to turn on me. When Jeezy decided it was "Fuck Gucci," a lot of dick riders seemed to fall in line out of fear of going against him and the crew he was running with. They were dominating Atlanta's nightlife, so DJs started cutting off "So Icy" before my verse. My reputation in the city went from rising star to one-hit wonder.

•

That lit a fire inside me. I was hustling at my homeboy's spot one day—when I wasn't recording I was trappin' heavy—and I'm hearing these niggas talk a whole bunch of junk about how Gucci Mane's finished, that I'd never have another big record. I sat there taking it all in, watching the scene at the dope spot unfold. I grabbed a pen and a napkin and started writing.

Choppa on the floor, pistol on the couch
Hood rich so I never had a bank account
Junkies going in, junkies going out
Made a hundred thou, in my trap house
Money kinda short but we can work it out
Made a hundred thou, in my trap house

Bricks going in, bricks going out
Made a hundred thou, in my trap house

—"Trap House" (2005)

I didn't even have a beat for this song but I knew it would be a hit. I decided then and there that I was no longer naming my debut album "So Icy." It would be called *Trap House* and it would silence all the naysayers. I was charged up and three weeks later, my debut album was complete.

Jeezy showed up to Charlie Brown Field for the video shoot but neither of us had anything left to say. He'd been trying to blackball me in the city and it worked. But I knew I'd just made a great album and soon that would get me back in the fanfare. I just wanted to get this video shoot over with and be done with the guy. I was over this shit.

But it wasn't over. At some point Black Magik took it upon himself to put out a whole bunch of songs dissing Jeezy, trying to use the Gucci-Jeezy beef to get himself some notoriety. Things were already bad, but when Magik put that shit on wax it added fuel to the fire. It also made everything public. There were no more whispers. Everything was out in the open and Jeezy was now in a spot where he really had no choice but to respond. But when he did, he didn't come at Magik. He came at me.

I was on the road headed out of town for a pair of shows in Florida when I heard "Stay Strapped" on the radio. Jeezy talked a lot of shit on there, but it was something he said at the end that really got my attention. Something about how he had ten grand for whoever brought him my "So Icy" chain.

I remember at first I was just pissed that he was calling my chain some bullshit. I'd paid forty thousand dollars for that piece. Now folks were going to see me rocking it and might think it was fake. But then it hit me. If it was open season on my chain, it was open season on me. There was another bounty on my head.

IX

SPRINGSIDE RUN

This part has to be brief. There are some things I can never really talk about.

I wrote "Round 1," my response to "Stay Strapped," in the car coming back from Tampa. As soon as I got back to Atlanta I went to the studio to record it. Black Magik ended up coming by to tack on a verse. I wasn't a fan of how Magik had involved himself in my and Jeezy's fallout, but that didn't matter anymore. I was at war and outnumbered. I needed all the allies I could get.

The dope game hard
The rap game easy
This is Round 1 of Gucci Mane vs. Jeezy
Gucci Mane vs. Jeezy
This is Round 1 of Gucci Mane vs. . . .
The East Atlanta boss

Dirty South like Slim Thugga
Jeezy couldn't make a hit with a Louisville Slugga
Slapped Coach K, pissed on Slick Pulla
Punched Kinky B dead in his dick sucka
Poppin' on the radio
Boy that's a bitch thang
Ridin' round with HB, smokin' on the cheap junk
Played you out a verse 'cause I know you was a big crab
Made Lil' Will sing the hook for a 50 slab
Did investigations, now I know ya background
Heard you from Hawkinsville
30 Miles from Mac Town
Think you got a buzz 'cause you known at Strokers?
Got 3 deals but the nigga still local
The dope game hard
The rap game easy
This is Round 1 of Gucci Mane vs. Jeezy
Gucci Mane vs. Jeezy
This is Round 1 of Gucci Mane vs. . . .
You a perfect example of what a crab is
Choppa hit ya make ya scream out ya ad-libs
Yeaaaaaahhhh, let's get it
Gucci voice on it then the hood gon' feel it
That 645 he leasin' it
In "Icy" video wearin' Meechy shit
3 cents off a album what Jeezy get
Put a dress on nigga you Meech's bitch
You a thug imposta, you deserve an Oscar
Album ain't hot, Def Jam finna drop ya
Hangin' round the Ball Park, claimin' you from Boulevard

Old ass Ferrari, you bought that shit from Pull-A-Part
Nothin' to lose, nothin' to prove
Might as well beef with ya, nothin' betta to do
Think ya on 'cause you probably sold a bird or 2
Outside 285 no one has heard of you

Since I'd been out of town I already felt like I was late in responding to "Stay Strapped," so "Round 1" needed to get out right away. Ace, my DJ and road manager at the time, told me he'd handle circulating the diss to the clubs and radio stations, but I thought this was something I needed to go out and put in people's hands myself. I didn't want anyone thinking I was hiding out while my DJ went around doing my bidding.

"Chill out, Ace," I told him. "I'm just going to Blaze."

My buddy had been fucking this stripper who danced at a club on Moreland called Blazin' Saddles. This girl can be found in the album booklet of *Trap House*. She's one of the two naked girls cooking crack on the stove. So I knew her too and I wanted to see if she could get the DJs at Blaze to play "Round 1" and some other new songs I had. So me and my friend went over there.

We weren't at Blaze long before she and her friend invited us back to her place, a house located on a dead-end street in Decatur named Springside Run.

And that's where it happened.

RAPPER WANTED IN SLAYING TURNS SELF IN
—The Atlanta Journal-Constitution, May 20, 2005

An up-and-coming Atlanta rapper whose debut album hits record stores Tuesday was expected to turn himself in to DeKalb County authorities Thursday night on a murder charge. The rapper, known as Gucci Mane, is wanted by DeKalb police in a shooting last week that left one man dead.

RAPPER IS WANTED AFTER SHOOTING DEATH

— The Augusta Chronicle, May 20, 2005

DECATUR - A murder warrant has been issued for the rapper known as Gucci Mane in a May 10 shooting in which a man was found dead, an attorney said.

The 25-year-old rapper, whose real name is Radric Davis, was notified Wednesday that he was wanted by DeKalb County authorities for the shooting of Henry Clark, said his attorney.

RAPPER WANTED FOR DEKALB MURDER SURRENDERS

— WSB-TV, May 20, 2005

Attorney for Man Says Shooting Was Self-Defense.

DECATUR - The rapper known as Gucci Mane turned himself in Thursday night after a murder warrant was issued for him in a May 10 shooting in which a man later was found dead.

ATLANTA RAPPER GUCCI MANE FACES MURDER CHARGE

— MTV, May 25, 2005

"Icy" Rapper Turned Himself in on Thursday, Claims He Fired in Self-defense.

X

THERE'S BEEN A MURDER

I was in New York City on set at BET's *Rap City* when they told me. *Trap House* was set to come out the following week.

For years I had imagined being a guest on *Rap City* and getting the chance to freestyle on *Tha Basement*. Now here I was, performing on TV, days away from the release of my debut album. I signed my name on the wall of the booth bigger than anyone else's. I wanted everyone who stepped inside to see it. But my dream come true transformed into a nightmare when I walked off the set.

•

"We need to get you back to Atlanta," Jacob told me. "There's a murder warrant out for your arrest."

There's no *good* time to find out you're wanted for murder, but learning like that, right there on the set of *Rap City*, fucked me up. There it was, right on the TV for everyone at BET to see:

Gucci Mane was a murder suspect. Moments earlier I'd been on such a high, proud of myself, but the rug had been pulled out from under me.

Jacob took a flight back to Atlanta but I drove back with my buddy Throw, Ace, and my security guard. We wanted to avoid a scene at the airport in case the police tried to scoop me there.

That was a long, quiet drive. First we stopped in New Jersey to pick up weed and get White Castle burgers. That was my first time eating White Castle. Then we headed home.

I was smoking like a chimney the whole ride. We were burning so much that we had to find more by the time we reached Washington, DC. We also made it a point to stop at a few strip clubs on the way and fuck some hoes too. But all that was a diversion from the reality of my situation.

I was sitting there in the backseat of that smoke-filled sedan, high as a jaybird, with John Legend's "Ordinary People" playing over and over and over again. That was my favorite song at the time.

My nerves grew as we approached Georgia, knowing what awaited me.

"Let's run, Throw," I suggested at one point. "Let's hide out in Alabama."

"You can't run, bro." He laughed. "You're too famous now. But don't worry, we'll beat this shit."

I wasn't so sure. Not a lot of people walked away from murder charges where I came from.

When we got to Atlanta we drove straight to the DeKalb County Jail; in the parking lot I met the attorney Jacob and Cat hired for me. He was an ex-cop turned defense attorney.

"Can you beat it?" I asked. Part of me still wanted to make a run for it.

"It's going to take a lot," he said. "But we can beat it."

Our brief meeting was interrupted by the flash of cameras. The media had arrived and Channel 2 Action News wanted to know what I had to say for myself.

"He's not going to say anything, okay?" my attorney told them. "He's a murder suspect and I'm his lawyer and I'm not going to let him say anything. Basically what happened, to make a long story short, he visited a young lady, went over to her place. She was there, he was there. At one point she opened up a door. Five guys come running in. One of them had green tape. One of them had a weapon. One of them had brass knuckles and hit him with the brass knuckles, hit him real hard. The other guy who had a weapon hit the other guy with a weapon. It became a situation where he defended himself. One of the five guys yelled 'Shoot him,' or something to that effect. He grabbed a gun that was nearby and opened fire. He defended himself. It was just him and a girl in there and five guys came in there to hurt him."

"It sounds like he was set up, then?" a reporter asked.

"I talked to a detective," my attorney told him. "The detective indicated he was set up. We have an independent witness we tried to give to the detective. The detective basically doesn't want a whole lot more information. We have a witness, a man who saw the five men go in. A woman, the young lady whom he was with, basically said she set him up. We're not sure of all the other facts yet."

With that, I headed inside and turned myself in to DeKalb County police for the murder of some twenty-seven-year-old dude. They told me he was from Macon. They told me he was a rapper too. I'd never met the man or even once heard his name.

I was wearing a T-shirt with a photo of Dr. Martin Luther King Jr. on it. Above his image it read, "I Have a Dream."

PART TWO

XI

DEKALB TO FULTON

"Round II"
    (written in an isolation cell in DeKalb County Jail)

I know I have my mother's luv
I know she's prayin' 4 me
But all the things I took her thru
I know it's hard 2 luv me
My older brother's disappointed
My little brother's scared
Been faced with trials my whole life
Yet still I'm not prepared
I always dreamed to be a rapper
Just like Big Daddy Kane
But all I got was jealousy
Since I took my daddy's name

I once lost my sanity
With prayer I got it back
My granddad had a heart attack
And we can't bring him back
I love my girl with all my heart
Though we both have made mistakes
Besides God no one's perfect
No one will ever take her place
My homeboys truly miss me
I cry because I miss 'em
I know they all can feel my pain
Them being victims of this system
Now as I write this poem
Tears are rushing down my cheeks
I want to be a respected black man
Like Big Cat and Frank Ski
They say I'm not intelligent
Because I have a speech impediment
But all that is irrelevant
Because my words are heaven sent
They say that I'm a murderer
But I do not believe it
So pray tonight for Gucci Mane
And even pray for Jeezy

—by Gucci Mane

•

Five days later I walked out of DeKalb County Jail on a hundred-thousand-dollar cash bond. It was May 24, 2005. *Trap House* was in stores and it was time to promote. But nobody was interested in talking about the album.

While I was locked up, the in-house publicist at Big Cat implemented a "crisis management campaign," issuing statements on my behalf.

"As much as I want to be celebrating my album release party rather than sitting alone in a cell where I don't belong, I can't feel sorry for myself because a man lost his life," said one.

"As a God-fearing person, I never wanted to see anyone die," read another. "I found myself in a predicament and even though there was an attack on my life, I truly never intended to hurt anyone, I was just trying to protect myself."

I didn't handle the questions as well upon my release, when I had to face them in person. I still hadn't had time to process the events of that night let alone be able to discuss them with strangers.

"Ain't too many people that got the motive to do some shit like that," I told Mad Linx, a few weeks after everything went down, on *Rap City*. "I just look at it like a detective, who has the motive to do it, and this fuck nigga is the only nigga that have motive."

"Jeezy?" Mad Linx asked.

"Yeah, straight up. I guess he's scared of competition. I'm independent. He's major. What the hell you beefin' with me for? Why would you jeopardize everything you got going to beef with a nigga at an independent label? There's something that I'm doing that he likes."

In a lot of folks' eyes I'd done some gangsta shit and people started rocking with me again for that. But I'd never walked around acting like I was hard. My music had always been fun because I'd always been a fun person. But now I had this reputation that I'd never sought out, something that was forced on me. And it wasn't only that my reputation had changed, the experience changed me too. I felt different. I was doing my best to keep everything going but in reality I was shell-shocked.

But the show had to go on. *Trap House*'s success or failure didn't only affect me. There was a lot on the line for a lot of people. So I carried on, hitting the road for my scheduled tour dates, doing performances in a bulletproof vest.

I knew when I walked out of DeKalb County after making bond that my newfound notoriety was going to be bad. Ultimately it was. To law enforcement and the press and the general public I would never catch a break on anything from that point on. But it wasn't hurting the release of *Trap House*, which was exceeding all expectations of what an independent album could do.

Two months after I turned myself in for murder, I touched down in Miami for a performance that Cat and Jacob booked for me at the downtown club Warehouse. As soon as we pulled up and stepped out of the car, all hell broke loose.

Everyone standing outside the club—the bouncers, valet parking attendants, patrons—turned to us with automatic weapons drawn. Every single one of them. It was a scene out of a movie.

"ATF! FBI! DEA! Everybody on the ground!"

It happened so fast I didn't have a chance to react. Before I knew it I was in the back seat of a black sedan, squeezed between four strangers. They hit the gas and sped off, without reading me my rights. Not a word was spoken. I thought I'd been kidnapped.

I realized I wasn't when we got to Miami's FBI headquarters minutes later. I was led to a conference room where the walls were covered with photos from huge drug busts, showcasing piles of seized bricks, guns, and money.

Two agents explained that they'd been made aware of death threats against me. Then they started asking about BMF and what I knew about the organization.

"Lawyer," I told them. "I ain't got nothing to say. Look, I'm tired. I need to go to sleep."

That was all I needed to say. I think maybe they couldn't question me after I said that because then anything I said would be under duress or something. I don't know. But I really was tired. It was the middle of the night and the experience of getting ambushed again like that had drained me. It was a shot of adrenaline when it happened but now I was crashing. I was taken to another room where I sat down on the floor and fell asleep.

When I woke up I was told there was a warrant out on me for an aggravated assault charge out of Fulton County back home. But why would the feds come down to Miami to serve a state warrant out of Georgia? Then I remembered all their questions about BMF.

As for this aggravated assault warrant, I wasn't sure what they were talking about. But when one of the agents mentioned a pool stick I realized.

This nigga who worked in promotions at the label had been booking shows in my name and pocketing the money. After I caught wind of this me and my boys found him at Big Cat's studio, and you can guess what happened. Allegedly a pool stick was involved.

I was to be extradited back to Georgia. I was crushed. Cat and Jacob had shown up to the office and I couldn't even look them in the eye. I stood there, my head hung, as the agents put me in cuffs.

Damn. This shit fucked up.

"Hey!" Cat shouted as they walked me out. "Put your mother-fucking head up."

I was taken to a local Miami PD precinct, where I was booked before being transferred to another jail. Two days later I was on a bus to Georgia.

I sat on that bus for two days as it stopped at damn near every correctional facility between Miami and Atlanta. It was the worst discomfort I'd ever felt. My wrists were in handcuffs and my ankles were shackled in leg irons. I couldn't move a muscle. The metal dug into my limbs and my whole body was cramping up. There I sat, captive, for miles on end. I got to use the bathroom once. Getting sleep was out of the question. It was crazy to me that you could do this to a person who hadn't even been convicted of a crime.

But Cat telling me to keep my head up stuck with me. I knew if I could just get through this temporary pain that tomorrow could bring a better day. That mentality would serve me in the years that followed.

•

I haven't exactly tested out every jail in the country, but I can tell you there ain't too many places like Fulton County. That place has got to be one of the most fucked-up correctional facilities in the United States.

Fulton County Jail was not like DeKalb County, where I'd

just spent a week before making bond on my murder charge and done my sixty-seven days back in 2002. DeKalb was heavily policed, with a bunch of old, white, racist good ol' boy COs running the show. They *love* fucking with niggas in there.

Fulton County is the city jail, policed by young black COs, many of whom came up in the same areas as the inmates. It is *very* easy to get a job there. Fulton County is not a place people aspire to work.

It was extremely overcrowded. Built in the eighties, the facility was designed to hold 1,332 inmates. When I got to Rice Street in '05, there were about three thousand of us in there. Cells meant to hold two bunks had three. Even that wasn't enough. There were mattresses strewn across the dayroom floor.

Bringing in some extra bunks and mattresses was easy, but they weren't adding showers and toilets to accommodate the overpopulation. The strain on the utilities resulted in system failures. Electric. Plumbing. HVAC. All fucked up. The overworked and understaffed maintenance workers couldn't keep up. It made for horrifying conditions.

Pipes were leaking. Toilets were overflowing. Sinks were clogged. Power outages were commonplace. The laundry machines didn't work, so inmates would wash their clothes in the shower, hanging them out to dry on the railings of the dayroom. The wet clothing only worsened the already unsanitary climate inside the pods, which were terribly hot and humid from the busted ventilation systems and crowded bodies. Mold was everywhere. And the smells. As if the food itself wasn't hard enough to put down, those fucking smells made it nearly impossible.

The inmates ran the show here and the place was rampant

with gangs, drugs, weapons, and corruption. The rule of law in Fulton County was simple. Anything goes.

•

I hadn't been there a month before I nearly caught a second murder charge.

I was still on and off with Danielle and she came by to see me a few weeks after I got locked up. I was on my way to visitation when I was blindsided. I don't know what the guy hit me with—maybe it was a lock?—but whatever it was, I was hit hard.

My ears were ringing. My vision was blurry. I was barely conscious. As I slowly came to, I was able to grab ahold of whatever it was he'd hit me with and we began to struggle over the metal object. We both had one hand on it and with our free hands we were blasting away at each other. A couple of punches later and this nigga was knocked the fuck out.

I'd gotten my wits about me by this point and was now fully enraged. Even though he was asleep I stayed swinging. I grabbed his legs and dragged him to the nearby stairwell. I was readying to throw him down the steps and break his neck. But then somebody saved my life and his.

"Don't throw him down those steps, man. You already won the fight."

I turned around to find an older inmate standing there who had seen the whole thing. This all happened right by visitation, so there were witnesses.

"Look, you're going to beat that murder charge," he told me. "Don't get another one. Just let him go."

So I did. With one tooth knocked out and blood pouring out my mouth, I walked down the same steps that I was about to throw my attacker down and extended my arms for the COs to put me in handcuffs. I was immediately brought to solitary confinement.

In the hole they had me three doors down from Brian Nichols. I couldn't believe it.

Earlier that year he'd been in all the papers. This guy was on trial for rape and before his appearance in court he'd beaten a sheriff's deputy damn near to death and taken her gun. Then he went into the courtroom, where he shot and killed a judge and a court stenographer. Outside he shot and killed another sheriff's deputy. He carjacked someone and a manhunt ensued. This was on *America's Most Wanted* and everything. While on the run, he killed a federal agent too. Eventually this lady he'd taken hostage convinced him to turn himself in.

How the hell could they have me in the same place as this guy? I'd just been on my way to visitation when someone attacked me. And I end up in solitary on some bullshit.

But I was treated just like Brian, stuck in my cell twenty-three hours a day. No windows. One bed. One sink. One toilet. The only light I saw was fluorescent. The air was stale. The only time I was allowed to leave was to use the shower, when I'd get escorted in shackles by a team of armed SWAT-like COs. When I got to use the phone they'd wheel it down on a cart to my cell and put the receiver through the same metal flap in the door that they put my food through. It was so inhumane. I started to lose it.

When I first got charged with the murder, I knew it was going to be a challenge but I also felt at the end of the day there was no way I could be convicted. I knew the facts of the case and that I hadn't been in the wrong that night. I'd done a lot of dirty, low-down things over the years, but what happened that night wasn't one of them. That's just all there was to it.

But the hole started fucking with me. With no human contact the only person I could talk to was myself, and I was saying crazy things, over and over again until I believed them. My thoughts became consumed by how many people had gotten convicted for murders they hadn't committed. More and more I started thinking that my life could be over. Over what? Nothing. Some song.

I was angry. Directly or indirectly this guy had put me in a situation where I had to fight for my life in the streets, and now I was going to be fighting for my life in the courts. Meanwhile he was out there enjoying all the success of his debut album. As the days turned to weeks and weeks turned to months I sat in solitary, going over how everything had played out. How had this good situation turned out so bad?

The more I thought about it, the more I started thinking maybe he resented me even before I turned Def Jam down. Prior to "So Icy" Jeezy was the new dude in Atlanta. He was riding with Meech and them and they were pulling up to the clubs in Gallardos and Phantoms and Bentleys and spending so much money it was unbelievable. But believe it. All those stories are true. I saw it with my own eyes.

But then here I was, creeping into what he thought was his limelight. I would understand those feelings if it weren't for the fact that I always thought we were coming from different angles. I wasn't talking about Lambos and Maybachs. I was rapping for the young boys on the corner with dirty T-shirts on. The ones cooking up in the kitchen. The car thieves. The shooters. The niggas breaking into houses. I was rapping *my* reality.

And I'd done it independently. I'd had help along the way from partners like Doo Dirty and Jacob and Cat. I'd had people like Clay Evans and DJ Greg Street from V-103 who took an interest in my career and looked out for me. But I hadn't come out of the major-label system and in a way that had made me the people's champ.

Maybe that fucked with his ego. Maybe he started viewing me as his competition, a thorn in his side. I'd never viewed him that way. Remember, I'd never even heard of the dude prior to our phone call through Shawty Redd, but he'd sure as hell heard of me. He was in south Georgia listening to "Muscles in My Hand" back in 2002. Maybe because I wasn't in awe of him, I never put on the shoes that he wanted me to wear. Maybe my keeping "So Icy" for myself was just the straw that broke the camel's back.

Or maybe being in the hole was just fucking with me.

Nearly three months after being placed in solitary confinement I caught the attention of the warden, who was walking through the wing.

"Can you tell me why y'all still got me in here?" I shouted.

She stopped, turned around, and approached my cell.

"Well, you stabbed your visitation buddy in the face," she responded.

"I did what?"

I still don't even understand how this shit happened but apparently I hit this guy so hard that his incisors went through his jaw on both sides of his mouth. When they took him to Grady Hospital he told them the reason he had these holes in his jaw was that I'd stabbed him in the face with a pen.

I explained to the warden that I hadn't stabbed anyone and she agreed to go back and check the surveillance footage. She returned the next day.

"Well, you're right," she told me. "We looked back at the footage and you didn't stab him. But let me ask you something else. Why were you still hitting him after he was unconscious?"

I didn't have an answer for that one but I wouldn't need one. After spending more than three months in solitary I was allowed to return to general protective custody. I had a disheveled Afro and a beard like T. J. Duckett. I was a mess. The hole had broke me down.

It seemed like there was little progress being made on my cases so I fired my attorney. Jacob was telling me that he had taken an aggressive approach with the DA, which had brought things to a standstill. So I hired a new team of lawyers from the law firm that had represented Baltimore Ravens linebacker Ray Lewis when he'd gotten charged with murder after an incident at a Super Bowl party in Atlanta in 2000. That case was a whole lot more complicated than mine, so I was hoping they'd be able to figure my shit out.

And they did. Things started moving after the new lawyers came aboard. They met with the Fulton County prosecutor and were able to find common ground. As far as the DA was concerned, their plaintiff wasn't the best victim. They knew this guy was a thief and had been stealing. At this point all he wanted was for his medical bills to be paid for. I was going to have to do some time for the assault, but this was a resolvable case.

But we still had a murder charge to deal with. My attorneys met with the DeKalb County assistant district attorney to review my case. They left that meeting with the understanding that my murder charge was soon going to be dismissed. They didn't have anything on me because of course they didn't. There was nothing to have.

The thing was the DA's office had a bunch of high-profile

cases and investigations going on at the time, and because they saw loose connections to mine they didn't want to drop my charges publicly yet. But off the record, we were told, I'd beaten the murder. This was months before that news became public.

It was relief more than it was happiness. A weight had been lifted off my shoulders, one that I'd forgotten I was carrying because it'd been there so long.

In October I pleaded no contest to my aggravated assault case. I was given a six-month sentence with six and a half years' probation. I'd already spent three months in Fulton County, so by the top of 2006, I was home.

XII

THE TRAP

The good news was I was free. The bad news was I'd spent a hell of a lot of money to get free. Fighting my two cases had drained my resources. Hiring and firing lawyers and the whole legal process had cost me over two hundred thousand dollars. I was damn near starting over.

Despite my absence, *Trap House* had been a huge success. My debut album had sold more than 150,000 copies independently. But somehow I wasn't seeing any of that money. Big Cat and Jacob told me of all these expenses they covered while I was away, but those expenses sounded more like excuses. Lame ones. The numbers weren't adding up.

As I was coming home Cat was readying to go in for a year. He'd had a strap on him the night we all got picked up in Miami and caught a charge being a convicted felon in possession of a firearm. He was going to have to do fourteen months in the feds.

Because he would be locked down for over a year, Cat wanted to get the ball rolling on my next album, which was ready to go. I'd recorded it prior to getting locked up and Jacob had come up with the title *Hard to Kill*. As soon as I got home there were interviews and phoners lined up to promote the album. But before I could do that, Cat and I needed to settle up.

I'd learned a lot in my time working with Cat. About what it took to put out a successful independent album. About publishing sheets. About accounting. Cat is someone I credit for making me a better businessman, but all the shit he taught me was about to bite him in the ass. I wanted to see the QuickBooks spreadsheets. I wanted to see the receipts. I needed a detailed explanation of the financials.

In addition to the album royalties I was owed, I'd also given him some money to hold on to before I went in. Now I needed that money back. I was broke.

Cat didn't have my money. He told me he needed a few days to get the money out of the bank and he offered me his credit card to use in the meantime. That was not what I wanted to hear.

"What the fuck do I want your credit card for?" I barked. "Where is my money?!"

I stormed out of the office and hit up one of my homeboys for a grand to hold me over. Later that night I had a performance lined up that would pay me seventy-five hundred, so I knew I wouldn't be broke for long. I was just pissed that Cat had set up all this shit but couldn't have my money for me. I'd asked him about it repeatedly. But like every other time I brought up money, it seemed, Cat had an excuse.

I came back to the Big Cat office a few days after the argument to meet with Jacob about my probation. Part of my plea deal was

I had all these community service hours I needed to fulfill. Even before I'd taken the plea I'd been thinking about how I wanted to give back after I got out. This was something I'd made a promise to myself to do if I beat my murder case. So I was all for it when Jacob told me he'd brought someone on board to help me get this nonprofit idea off the ground. This was the day I got introduced to Deborah Antney. Like Cat and Jacob, Deb was a transplant from New York. She'd been living in Georgia for the last decade but still had a thick Queens accent. Her background was in social services but she'd recently worked with a few well-known recording artists on setting up their foundations and different charity ventures.

Deb and I discussed what I was looking to do. I explained I wanted to organize a back-to-school giveaway of sorts, where we'd hand out new book bags full of school supplies to kids in Zone 6. The conversation went well, but before we parted ways she pulled me aside.

"Listen, these people don't have your best interests at heart," she told me. "That's what they brought me in for. I don't want any part of it but I just thought I should let you know."

What Deb was telling me was what I was already suspicious of. And while I still wasn't quite sure of what to make of this lady, I did know I was about finished dealing with Big Cat and Jacob.

Later that week I was on the set of a video shoot for "Go Head," one of the songs off *Trap House* that had blown up while I was locked up. Deb was there and so was Jacob. But I wasn't interested in speaking with either of them. The only thing on my mind was the money I was owed and the things Deb had told me the other day. I left the set and decided that I was done doing business with these people. "Go Head" never did get a music video.

•

My departure from Big Cat would trigger my return to the streets. It wasn't long before I was knee-deep in it again, running with my old partners. Time had healed old wounds and everyone was still doing what they'd been doing. It was back to trappin' like we had been.

My homeboys had a new spot they were operating out of and it soon became mine as well. There were a couple of niggas who actually lived there but mostly this was a trap house to juug out of. The type of place where the lights would go out and we'd have no power but we still wouldn't leave the house. Or the refrigerator would stop working and we'd send one of the young boys to the store to get us drinks. Or the stove went out and we'd get someone to turn the gas back on illegally. It was a hangout too. Smoking, gambling, and girls. But when the pack came in it was down to business.

Given the success I'd had in the music game, it was crazy how quick I was back to the same shit. It was like I never stopped. But my attitude had become "Fuck Music." Big Cat had put out this song "My Chain" as the first single to *Hard to Kill* and the response to it was lukewarm. People weren't really feeling it. "My Chain" is a cool song but looking back on it now, Zay and I may have been trying too hard to re-create the magic of "So Icy" with another song about jewelry.

Paired with the fact that I was at odds with my label, I was feeling like the rap game had brought me more problems than the streets ever had. People were telling me that I needed to get back to the music but I wasn't into it. *Hard to Kill* was finished. Let Big Cat put it out and we'd go from there.

This would become a trend throughout the course of my career. Whenever the music wasn't going right I would fall back into the streets. Maybe it was a coping mechanism. Going back to something I knew I'd find success in when I wasn't experiencing it elsewhere. Whatever it was, it was a habit that went on for much longer than you'd think.

•

The trap house was boomin' one day when my buddy ran inside and grabbed me. His urgency caught me off guard.

"Man, you ain't gonna believe who's outside," he told me.

"Who?" I asked.

"Your momma."

He was right. This was unbelievable.

For one, Mother Dearest and I had not been on good terms for a while. We'd had a rocky relationship ever since she kicked me out of the house in '01. But that's not even what was fucking me up. I just couldn't believe she was actually *here*, at my trap. My momma didn't do shit like that. She wouldn't be caught dead in a place like that. This house had been shot up days earlier. Junkies were coming in and out as the hours passed.

Standing next to my momma was Deb Antney. She'd been on a mission to get in touch with me ever since the failed "Go Head" video shoot. Somehow she found my mother, who had caught wind of what I was up to.

"What are you doing here?!" I asked them. I was in shock.

"We want to talk to you," Deb explained. "You're throwing your life away. You have a real chance to make it. Why would you be back here doing this?"

At first I couldn't get past the fact that my momma was actually standing outside. But after they left, Deb's words took root. I'd just gotten out of jail. Maybe I shouldn't be doing this. At the very least I should get back to working on my music too. But I wasn't going back to Big Cat.

•

One of the people who helped me get back to working on music was Shawty Lo. I was walking through the South DeKalb Mall one day when I saw a dude who had on as much jewelry as I did. The nigga stood out. When I peeped his chain I realized he was in the rap group D4L.

D4L was a rap crew out of the Bowen Homes projects in Bankhead, a neighborhood on the Westside of Atlanta. Zone 1. They were the pioneers of snap music and at the top of 2006 snap music had taken over the country. "White Tee," the Dem Franchize Boyz song that inspired "Black Tee," had been the beginning of snap, but D4L had brought it to the masses. Their song "Laffy Taffy" hit Number 1 on the Billboard charts the month I came home from prison.

But I wasn't familiar with Shawty Lo. I'd been locked up during D4L's rise and Lo wasn't even on "Laffy Taffy" or "Betcha Can't Do It Like Me," their other big song. Lo wasn't on most of the songs on their album. This guy was what I'd originally set out to be: a hustler turned financier who hopped on a track every now and then. Like me, Lo had just come home from a year in prison. He was a real street nigga and we hit it off.

Lo had his own studio in Bankhead, and as our friendship developed he told me I could record there for free. Since I was no longer recording at Big Cat's studio and now had to foot the bill myself for studio time, I took him up on his offer. I started going there a lot. He had a whole roster of in-house producers who hooked me up with beats too.

That meant something to me. Lo didn't need anything from me. He extended his hand, asking for nothing in return. He had character, he was a genuine person. Ever since then we were close friends. I was there for Lo for anything. A cameo in a video, a feature, whatever it was. I could never charge him a dollar.

Then there was this white kid, DJ Burn One, who had been trying to get me to do a mixtape with him ever since "Black Tee." Burn One was still in high school but he was serious about the mixtape game. When I met him he'd been putting together compilation tapes of songs from artists he liked, but now he wanted to do tapes exclusively with one artist, like how DJ Drama was doing with *Gangsta Grillz*.

I ran into Burn One not long after my stint in Fulton County but had brushed him off. *Trap House* had been a big success and *Hard to Kill* was going to be a bigger one. What did I need to do a mixtape for?

But things had changed. I didn't know what the situation was with *Hard to Kill* and "My Chain" hadn't taken off. I was back to selling dope and the more I thought about it, maybe I *was* back to square one. Maybe doing a mixtape wasn't such a step backward.

I hit up Burn One and met him at Zay's, where I was knocking out a verse for some niggas I'd met at a club called Blue Flame. It was four in the morning by the time Burn One showed up, but I'd taken two X pills and was wide awake. I was geekin' that night.

With some convincing, Zay let us all in his basement. Middle-of-the-night surprise sessions were not his thing, but these guys were going to pay him for a beat, so he obliged. Zay played a few cuts and after these dudes found one that was to their liking, I laid down my verse. Then it was time for the other guy to do his.

This nigga rapped the worst shit I'd ever heard in my life. It was terrible. And when he walked out I told him so.

"That sucked," I told him straight up. "I can't be next to you on that. Burn One, you want my verse? You can have it."

Burn One didn't say a word. He could see these guys were pissed.

"What are you talking about?" the other one asked. "We just paid you five thousand dollars for that verse."

"Nah, the five thousand was for Zay's beat," I told them. "I can't give you my verse."

I switched the script. As lame as these dudes were with music, they weren't soft. I'd seen guns in their car. Even as things got tense I wouldn't budge. I was all over the place. Zaytoven saw where this was going, so he decided to cut his losses and wipe his hands of the situation. We were told to leave.

The arguing continued outside and the way shit was going this would end one of two ways. Either the cops were getting called or someone was getting shot. Burn One, who hadn't spoken since I offered him the verse for free, butted in, sensing I wasn't going to be the one to deescalate the situation.

"Let's just all go to the strip club and we'll sort this out there."

Somehow that worked. I got into Burn One's little red pickup truck and we took off.

"Man, I ain't goin' back to Blue Flame," I told him.

He already knew that and he hit the gas and we dipped, leaving those fellas high and dry and out of five grand.

During that drive Burn One put me up on game about the mixtape circuit. It was a whole different ecosystem with a lot less rules and red tape when compared to putting out an album. He told me about all this money that artists were making from their mixtapes. To me, it seemed, this could be the route to get my career back on track.

The sun was starting to come up by the time Burn One dropped me off at my place. I put a couple of hundred dollars in his hand before we parted ways.

"Thanks for that shit back there," I told him. "We'll start doing the mixtape tomorrow."

Over the next few weeks me and Burn One cooked up *Chicken Talk,* my first mixtape. It was a wild period of time. I kept my little run with the X pills going and you can hear it in those songs. It made for great music. More than any other release of mine *Chicken Talk* captured my state of mind during the time I was making it. I dissed every single Big Cat artist on that shit. It's a perfect time capsule and my favorite of all my mixtapes.

After we got *Chicken Talk* pressed up, me and Burn One went to the Old National Flea Market to sell some copies. The guy there wasn't having it.

"Ain't nobody gonna buy that," he told Burn One. "I heard Gucci Mane over with."

Meanwhile I was outside in the parking lot with my new tape booming out of Burn One's truck. A small crowd had gathered around me and I was selling copies hand over fist. The guy inside, the same one who'd just told Burn One my career was finished, saw what was happening and ran out a couple of minutes later.

"Let me get forty of those," he said.

Chicken Talk got my buzz going again. Not only in Atlanta but through the South all the way up to the Midwest, where I developed a loyal following. Its success started getting me booked for shows in Detroit, Chicago, Pittsburgh, and every big city in Ohio. It gave me a needed boost, pushing me back on track.

Now I needed to find replacements for Cat and Jacob. Ever since that day at the trap house, Deb had begun loosely handling my business affairs and over time we became very close. She went from being Deb Antney to Auntie Deb. She had a nurturing way about her and she was protective of me during a time when I was still dealing with the aftermath of what happened in '05.

I knew Deb didn't know shit about the music business. I probably knew more than she did just from my dealings with Cat. But she had convinced me that she had my best interests at heart. At the time that's what I was looking for. Someone I could trust.

We both wanted to get me out of my deal with Big Cat, and Deb claimed to know someone who could make that happen. We took a trip to New York City to meet him.

James Rosemond, better known as Jimmy Henchman, was the CEO of the artist management company Czar Entertainment. His client list included the Game, Akon, Brandy, and Salt-N-Pepa. A couple of years back he'd negotiated the terms of Mike Tyson's fight against Lennox Lewis, one of the highest-grossing events in boxing pay-per-view history. Years later Jimmy was convicted of running a multimillion-dollar drug ring. He's now serving life. But at the time of our business I didn't know about any of that. I just knew his name held weight in the music business.

For a finder's fee, Jimmy could get me a new deal with one of the major labels and figure out a way to end my obligations to Cat. To oversee that he set me up with a new lawyer, Doug Davis, the son of the legendary music executive Clive Davis.

Meanwhile Big Cat had just released *Hard to Kill*, which was doing well despite its CEO being locked up and my lack of promotion. But "Go Head" was killing it in the clubs, and "Stupid," a song from *Chicken Talk*, was making noise too.

Two months after *Hard to Kill* dropped, Atlantic Records reached an agreement with Big Cat to buy out my contract. There's a lot more to that story, but the truth is it belongs more to the people who were heavily involved in the negotiations behind the scenes. All I knew was that I would be a major-label artist on Asylum Records, a subsidiary of Atlantic. And I'd have my own imprint, So Icey Entertainment, of which I'd own 66 percent and Deb would own 33 percent. Todd Moscowitz had finally gotten the artist he'd wanted and all ties were severed with my former label. At least I thought they were.

Part of going through Jimmy to get the deal at Asylum was that I'd work with a group of producers whom Czar Entertainment set me up with for my major label debut. These producers included Reefa, the guy who did the Game's "One Blood," Polow da Don, and a bunch of others I was unfamiliar with. They weren't my go-to producers. I wasn't thrilled about the arrangement, but I viewed it as a necessary sacrifice to get the new deal done.

One producer I was excited to work with was Scott Storch, whom I met shortly after I got my deal with Asylum. Scott was one of the hottest producers in the game. He had just made Fat Joe's "Make It Rain" with Lil Wayne, a huge hit. Word was Scotty was charging like a hundred thousand dollars a beat at the time, but because he really wanted to work with me he was only going to charge the label fifty thousand.

I met Scott Storch at the famed Hit Factory studios in Miami. He was in a session with another artist when I came by so we didn't get to any music that day. But we hit it off.

"Gucci, you cool as hell," he told me. "Why don't you come over for dinner tomorrow night?"

I'd heard Scotty lived lavish and liked to party, but I wasn't prepared for what I saw when I pulled up to his house.

Seventy Palm Avenue. Scotty was living in a ten-million-dollar mansion on Palm Island. Twenty thousand square feet. Nine bedrooms, seventeen baths.

Behind the gates were his cars. A 2007 Bugatti Veyron, black, fully loaded. An '05 Lamborghini Murciélago, white with red interior. A silver McLaren with butterfly doors. An '05 Ferrari 575 Superamerica, the red one from the "Make It Rain" video. An Aston Martin Vanquish S. A Rolls-Royce Phantom, drop-top. Another Phantom next to it. That was the front of the house.

To the side of the house were Scotty's old-schools. A 1960 Bentley S2. A 1973 Jaguar XKE. I can't remember them all. There must have been twenty foreign cars parked out there. Out back was *Tiffany*, his 120-foot yacht.

This was early in my career, but to this day I haven't really seen someone putting on the way Scotty was in that house. The guy was living like Scarface.

Inside he had some friends over when I came in with my girl. We sparked up a blunt and got to talking. Then he introduced me to his buddies.

"This is the guy I was telling you about!" he said excitedly.

"The guy who everybody don't like. You know, the one with the murder charge!"

My jaw almost hit the floor. This was not the way I wanted to be introduced. I gave Scotty a look, hoping he'd realize his mistake and change the subject, but it kept going. He and his crew of yes men having their own conversation about my life while I was standing right there in front of them.

What the fuck?

I looked over at my girl and she looked equally taken aback, which let me know I wasn't tripping over nothing. That was my cue to get out of there.

"Hey, homes," I interrupted. "I appreciate you having me over for dinner, but I'm out of here."

"What? What do you mean?" he said. "What's going on?"

He had no idea what he'd done to offend me. I later learned that there was a good chance Scotty was high as hell on the powder. I read somewhere he blew like thirty million dollars in six months on a cocaine bender for the history books. He ended up losing that mansion. Of course I didn't know that then. I just thought the guy was lame.

My mind was racing when I left that night and I wasn't even thinking about what he'd said. A lot of people were saying stupid shit like that upon meeting me. This was just a bad one.

Around the same time I met Rick Ross while I was down in Gainesville, Florida, for a show. A mutual friend of ours, a DJ by the name of Bigga Rankin, asked if I'd push back my flight home so that he could introduce us. Ross had just put out "Hustlin'" and was on his way to stardom. Bigga Rankin spoke highly of him.

"He's a smart guy, Gucci," he told me. "You guys should meet."

The first thing Rick Ross said to me didn't seem so smart.

"If I was you, every time I rapped I'd say 'I killed a nigga and got away with it.'"

Listen, both Scotty and Ross ended up being cool as hell and people I consider true friends and partners in this industry. I tell those stories just to show how people were looking at me then. Like a killer. I was having encounters like that all the time.

But again, I wasn't even thinking about any of that when I was walking out of Scotty's mansion. All I was thinking about was this house and this driveway full of cars and that yacht out back. I knew I needed to step my game up.

XIII

THE SO ICEY BOYZ

My major-label debut with Asylum would be titled *Back to the Trap House*. This is ironic because the album ended up being the total opposite of what I'd done with *Trap House*. Going "back to the trap house" would have meant locking back in with Zay and Shawty Redd. But despite its title, this album was meant to be something else entirely.

"We're taking you in a new direction," I was told. "This is what's going to bring you to that next level."

The initial plan was to run with "Bird Flu" as the lead single. "Bird Flu" was a record Zay produced, and of the songs that made the final track listing, I felt it was one of the better ones. I liked "16 Fever" too, but that's neither here nor there. "Bird Flu" was set to get a big push and for a minute it did. Then "Freaky Gurl" happened.

"Freaky Gurl" was a song from *Hard to Kill* that was inspired by my new white Hummer H2, one of the first big purchases I made with rap money. I'd recorded it a while back, after the making of *Trap House* but before I caught my two cases. The hook was a play on Rick James's classic "Super Freak."

She's a very freaky girl, don't bring her to mama
First you get her name, then you get her number
Then you get some brain in the front seat of the Hummer
Then you get some brain in the front seat of the Hummer

"Freaky Gurl" was not a song I'd given much thought to after recording it, so I was surprised to hear it was getting played on the radio, nearly two years after it was made.

Everything about its rise felt off to me. It wasn't organic. When "Black Tee" and then "So Icy" started buzzing in the city, I saw the impact of those songs. The way people would respond in the club when they came on, it was undeniable. I wasn't seeing that with "Freaky Girl" but the radio spins didn't lie and this old song was suddenly bringing me to that "next level" the folks from Asylum kept talking about getting me to. The streets embraced me after *Trap House* but "Freaky Gurl" was the song that got people's mommas aware of me. It was the "Back That Azz Up" to Juvenile's "Ha."

Now Asylum wanted "Freaky Gurl" but the song didn't belong to them. Publishing rights were owned by Big Cat Records. After everything that went down in '05, I had no interest in another squabble over the rights to a song. But behind the scenes this was a very big deal. A tug-of-war for the record ensued. Negotiations with Big Cat for the rights to "Freaky Gurl" went nowhere and the situation got even more complicated after "Pillz," *another* song off *Hard to Kill*, started to pick up steam.

Maybe the majors didn't know how to handle me as an artist. Even with all their muscle behind it, "Bird Flu" was being overshadowed by old songs that a small independent label out of the South were pushing. And instead of going back to the drawing board and reconsidering the approach to my upcoming album, Asylum decided the solution was to piggyback on the success of "Freaky Gurl" and "Pillz" and find a way to get them for themselves. Which they did. I rerecorded "Freaky Gurl" and the label put Ludacris and Lil' Kim on there. "Pillz" was renamed "I Might Be" and features from the Game and Shawnna got added on.

When the time came to turn in *Back to the Trap House*, I submitted two different albums to Asylum.

The first one was comprised of songs I'd done with the producers recommended to me as part of my deal with Czar Entertainment. I recorded most of those during a two-day visit to New York City. The second album I turned in had a bunch of superhard songs I'd made with Zay, Shawty Redd, and Fatboi, a producer from Savannah whom I'd started working with recently. This album had the songs "My Kitchen," "Vette Pass By," and "Colors." Songs that today are considered my classics. But in 2007 Asylum didn't like them.

They said they sounded like mixtape tracks, that they wouldn't make an impact beyond 285. They liked the album with all the other producers and the big-name features and commercial vibes. I didn't agree but I was trusting the people overseeing this album. These were the folks who'd promised this release would make me a superstar. So I ended up going with the first one. Those songs I'd made during that two-day trip to New York would be the nucleus of *Back to the Trap House*.

The album wasn't due to come out for a few months, but I

didn't have to wait until then to enjoy my success. With "Freaky Gurl" climbing the charts, I was feeling more and more like the star I wanted to be. I'd gotten the Hummer. I'd spent seventy-five thousand dollars on an iced-out Bart Simpson chain. When someone from *The Simpsons* complained and we had to blur out Bart in the "Freaky Gurl" videos due to creative licensing issues, I went out and got an Odie chain. But man, folks were really going crazy for that Bart chain. Every city I'd hit the club, promoters would ask me if I could wear it when I hit the stage.

•

After years of always being the young nigga in the crew, I now had a bunch of young niggas under me. OJ and I were super-tight then and at some point Deb had started bringing her son Waka around. Waka was not Waka Flocka Flame then. He was not a rapper. He was just a nineteen-year-old kid whose mother was really worried about him. Waka was not much of a hustler but he was gangbangin' hard with his boys in Clayton County. They're known for that kind of shit up there. Like getting into huge fights in the clubs and beefing with niggas they don't even know over little shit or nothing at all. Just crazy, wild, stupid shit. That's what Waka was up to. Deb had already lost a son under tragic circumstances, and the way Waka was going, it was only a matter of time before he got himself killed too. So I took him under my wing, along with his older brother, Wooh, and their cousin Frenchie. The So Icey Boys.

Deb purchased a big house in a subdivision of Eagle's Landing. For a while I stayed there too. I became a part of that family. There were good times and bad times in that house, but there was definitely a lot of love. Eventually I got my own house down the street and the boys came with me. There were a lot of good times there too. The So Icey Boys clubhouse.

Out of all 'em Waka was always the one who stood out. He wasn't from Atlanta, so people started wondering, who is Gucci's new goon? He started hangin' around me so much that people identified him with me, expecting him to always be by my side. Everyone called Waka my shooter, and he was, but he was a lot more than just muscle. He and I became incredibly close. Inseparable. Like brothers.

I remember Waka was in the studio with me while I was finishing up *Back to the Trap House*. I was working with Polow da Don on a song called "I Know Why." Waka had never rapped a verse in his life, but for some reason Polow gave him a look up and down and then turned to me.

"That dude who with you, Gucci," he told me. "I think he could be a star."

"You know what, Polow?" I said. "I been thought that."

XIV

MAKING THE MACHINE

Back to the Trap House debuted at number 57 on *Billboard*'s Top 200, selling fewer than thirty-two thousand copies in its first week. My major-label debut was a dud. I knew those beats were not suited to my style. I'd taken too much outside advice. I should have stood up for myself and put out the album I wanted.

The label planned on following the "Freaky Gurl" remix with "I Know Why," featuring Pimp C, Rich Boy, and Blaze1—the song Polow and I had been working on when he said Waka was going to be a star. But two weeks before the album came out Pimp C died. Something about a sleep apnea disorder, compounded by drinking lean.

My own habits with the stuff had gotten bad. Over the years there had been times when I'd gone too hard with the X pills, but that had always felt recreational. With the lean I'd developed a dependence. It became something I needed. My life was moving fast and this drink helped me slow everything down. I was now on the road nearly every weekend, which meant long bus rides of smoking weed and sipping lean to pass the time. I just wasn't as outward with my usage as a lot of other rappers were with the Styrofoam cups because I was still on probation.

In the beginning lean had been something special, a vice I enjoyed. An indulgence. Now it was something I required to operate. My fame was at an all-time high and these pints helped me calm down and relax in situations where I would otherwise feel anxious, like a big performance or a radio interview where I knew I'd get asked about some shit I didn't want to talk about.

A known side effect of codeine is constipation and all the drank sitting in my stomach had given me a gut. I didn't give a fuck. My little potbelly wasn't stopping these beautiful women from wanting to fuck me. The lean would have me so nonchalant and relaxed, it would only make them want me more.

•

After Pimp C died the label stopped pushing "I Know Why" as a single and after that the whole album fizzled out.

Things weren't all bad. Ever since the success of "Freaky Gurl" and "Pillz" I was getting booked for shows across the country. My fee was up to thirty thousand dollars a performance.

In December 2007, the weekend before *Back to the Trap House* came out, I was in Columbus, Ohio, opening for Lil Wayne on his Best Rapper Alive tour. I had my own tour bus by this point, but for whatever reason we were in a ten-passenger Sprinter van that day when we pulled into the parking lot of the Veterans Memorial Auditorium. Wayne had two huge tour buses parked nearby.

I hopped out of the van and was making my way toward the venue when I saw this pretty girl get off Wayne's bus and start running toward us. She was small, no taller than five-two, but right away I saw a big personality.

"Gucci! I always wanted to meet you," she said. "I'm Nicki, I'm here with Young Money."

She told me she was a fan and had even put out her own remix to "Freaky Gurl."

"Why would you put a bitch from Brooklyn on there, though?" she asked, referring to Lil' Kim. "I know you got people in Queens. You supposed to have a bitch from Queens on there."

For her to know my connections to Queens, she really must be a fan, I thought. This girl was cool. We exchanged numbers and I went inside to perform.

After the show I was back on the van, telling Waka and Frenchie about the interaction. Turned out they knew of her. Nicki Minaj. They'd seen her on one of *The Come Up* DVDs. They thought she was rolling with this New York dude Fendi and signed to his label Dirty Money Records. Apparently she was rolling with Young Money now.

I kept in contact with Nicki and over the next few months she started driving to Atlanta in her white BMW to work on music. Then I started flying her out, putting her up in hotels, until she eventually got a spot of her own.

Nicki had gotten a big look from her feature on Wayne's *Da Drought 3* mixtape, but outside of that she felt like the label wasn't taking her seriously. She wasn't happy with her management either. So I introduced her to Deb, who ended up signing her to her management company Mizay Entertainment. Later on I put her in touch with my partner DJ Holiday, who a year later would host her *Beam Me Up Scotty* mixtape, Nicki's break-through release.

People think I dropped the ball not signing Nicki, but from the day we met my understanding was that her loyalty was with Young Money and Wayne. I just saw a lot of talent, enjoyed work-ing with her, and wanted to help any way I could.

Speaking of Wayne, all my young niggas were always bring-ing his new mixtapes on the tour bus. It seemed like Wayne was putting out new shit every week. I fucked with Wayne's music but there was a part of me that didn't like that my protégés were on my bus, vibing to another nigga's music. They should've been listening to me. Except I wasn't recording like Wayne was, so I didn't have a whole lot of new songs to be playing on the long trips.

The disappointment of *Back to the Trap House* already had me feeling like I had something to prove. So I made up my mind. I would flood the streets with music too.

I hit up every DJ I knew and told them I wanted to do a mix-tape with them.

EA Sportscenter with Holiday, *Mr. Perfect* with DJ Ace, *So Icey Boy* with Supastar J. Kwik, *Ice Attack* with Dutty Laundry, *Wilt Chamberlain* with DJ Rell, *Gucci Sosa* with DJ Scream, *From Zone 6 to Duval* with Bigga Rankin.

I made plans to do all these projects, which meant I needed to start recording like hell. And that's what I did. When I wasn't on the road I was at Zay's house first thing in the morning. If I wasn't at Zay's, I was at Shawty Redd's. If I wasn't at Shawty's, then I was at Patchwerk with Drumma Boy. If I wasn't at Patch-werk, then I was at Fatboi's. The studios switched up but one thing remained constant: I was recording nonstop.

My decision to do all these mixtapes would change my entire approach to making music. Until that point I'd mostly written down my raps. Even when I was "freestyling" on the radio or how I did on *Rap City* back in '05, it was always me reciting something I'd written.

It was actually a few months before *Back to the Trap House* that I first experimented with changing things up. I was doing a mixtape called *No Pad No Pencil* with Supastar J. Kwik. As its title indicates, *No Pad No Pencil* had a bunch of freestyles on there.

At the time I was working on it I was also shooting a documentary with Hood Affairs. I thought it'd be a dope idea to shoot me in the booth, hearing beats for the first time and just going in on them off the top. I was working with a young producer by the name of Mike Will and I told him to keep feeding beats into my headphones. Then I got after 'em . . .

Let me tell you like . . .
It's just another day in the East Atlanta 6
Just a young nigga in the hood selling bricks
Just another nigga, just another clique
Just another girl, man you just another bitch
Just another day in the East Atlanta 6
You choosin' me so you on the dope man dick
Yellow Corvette, that's the dope man's drop
Blue and white Jacob that's the dope man's watch
Bouldercrest Road, that's the dope man's block
"Dope man! Dope man! Can I please cop?"
Police tryin' to tell the dope man "Stop"
The dope man thinkin' "man, I gotta make a knot"

The trap kinda slow, I'mma make the trap hot
Waka Flocka Flame, tell bro to bring the chopper
I'mma throw, throw ya back, back, back to '89
Moved to Atlanta, Georgia, I was just 9
Mountain Park Apartments, everybody on the grind
Then I moved to Sun Valley everybody had a 9
Went to school, 11, with a mothafuckin' knife
When I was 13, I got my first stripe
Got my first stripe, it's Gucci Mane LaFlare
Kush smokin', Dro smokin', put it in the air
Nigga this a Hood Affair, every hood, everywhere
When you hear this in yo car, you gon' want to pull a chair up
Gucci Mane LaFlare, I be ridin' in that Leer
I be so iced up, I be so kushed up
All I wanna do is be like Gucci when I grow up
All I wanna do is buy a pound and get dro'd up
All she wanna do is buy a ball and get snowed up
Tell her that I got her 'cause I know that she a shopper
Shawty want a 8-Ball, tell her call Waka
Shawty want a pound tell her Doe gotta her
I'm gonna serve her, chop her like a burger
Gucci Mane LaFlare and this track here murdered

—"East Atlanta 6" (2007)

I killed that shit! I'd just been trying to shake things up and do something different, but damn that came out hard. And I had so much fun doing it.

It wasn't a calculated decision to switch my whole style up, but months later, with these new projects in the pipeline and deadlines to meet, freestyling proved to be a much quicker way for me to knock out songs. So that's what I started doing and I did so relentlessly. I became a machine. I would record six or seven songs a day. Easily.

Even when I was writing raps down, my peers had trouble keeping up. That was something I'd first noticed in Zay's basement years before. We'd start work on a song and I'd have three verses and a hook done before Zay finished the beat. When I started working with other artists and producers it was the same. I set a pace that few could match.

Now that I was freestyling, no one stood a chance of keeping up. I certainly wasn't sitting around the studio waiting for anyone to catch up. One take. Play the next beat.

"Just track the drums and give me one sound," I started telling producers. "That's all I need."

A lot of rappers need to hear beats for inspiration, but I never showed up to the studio with nothing to say. If anything I had the opposite problem. I was overflowing with ideas, which was why I was rapping on these unfinished skeleton beats, to get one batch of ideas out of my system and be able to move on to the next.

Sitting still in the studio killed me. I couldn't do it. I always had something to get off my chest. I was always thinking about how I could phrase things in a way that would connect with folks. The producers could finish up the beats on their own time. You have no idea how many songs I made—big, well-known ones—that were nothing but a kick and a snare in my headphones when I recorded them.

My work ethic would pay off. With each mixtape I dropped, the disappointment surrounding *Back to the Trap House* faded away. I was getting hotter and hotter.

My mixtape run of 2008 would culminate with *The Movie*, with DJ Drama. Doing a *Gangsta Grillz* mixtape was always on my bucket list. But because of my issues with certain artists over the years I hadn't pursued it. I had a lot of respect for Drama and I didn't want to put him in a tough spot. Still, I always knew that we could put together something amazing.

Drama knew it too. He saw what was happening with my career. When the feds raided his studio in 2007 and he ended up in county jail for a night, niggas in there were telling him Gucci was the truth. Now every city he went to, people wanted to hear my music and he wasn't going to be the one to stop them. And he had fallen out with Jeezy. So when Drama reached out about doing a tape I didn't need to give it much thought. I'd been waiting on that call for years.

But before *The Movie* Drama and I teamed up for a mixtape called *Definition of a G* with Memphis rapper Yo Gotti. *Definition of a G* would serve as the announcement for the *The Movie*, setting the stage for something major to come. If Drama doing a tape with me wasn't the nail in the coffin for his and Jeezy's friendship, he made sure of it with a freestyle on the outro of *Definition of a G* where I rapped over the beat for "Put On," a Jeezy song.

"You asked for it!" Drama boomed. "Gucci *Gangsta Grillz* on the way!"

I think I hit a new peak making *The Movie*. These were some of my craziest flows to date. I was in a special zone creatively.

Shawty hotter than a hippopotamus in the Sahara
With a rump like a rhinoceros just like Toccara

An ass like ass-trologist I need a telescope
I asked her what's her Zodiac so I could read her horoscope
—"Bachelor Pad" (2008)

Drama did his thing on there too, sequencing the songs to put together one of my most cohesive releases. And he talked his shit throughout, sending little jabs and making *The Movie* a moment to remember.

You see, I used to be Sammy Jackson . . . Means I had too
many snakes on my plane . . . But now, I'm Jack Nicholson . . .
'Cause I'm shinin' on you niggas!!!
—"I'm a Star" (2008)

Unfortunately I'd miss that moment. One week before *The Movie* came out I went in front of a Fulton County judge for a probation violation hearing. I'd gotten arrested over the summer. After a late night I was driving back to Eagle's Landing with a couple of girls when I hit a sobriety checkpoint. The officer said he smelled weed, which gave him probable cause to check the car. Before I knew it I was charged with possession of marijuana, DUI, and possession of a firearm by a convicted felon.

I'd pissed dirty a couple of times too. So there was reason to revoke my probation at that hearing. But I couldn't believe it when I heard my violation was that I'd only completed twenty-five of my six hundred required community service hours.

This was some bullshit. I had been doing the community service. My probation officer was this supercool white lady. She cared a lot about the kids of Atlanta and thought I could be a role model to them. So I'd been going to schools with her and talking to the young ones about staying out of trouble. We organized a shoe drive too.

What happened was her supervisor didn't approve of the community service I'd been doing. This guy wanted me out on the highway picking up trash or something. Really what he wanted was for me to do something that would embarrass me, humble me, something that would knock me down a peg. But my probation officer had been there with me at all those schools. This was the one part of my probation that I'd been on top of. I couldn't believe this shit.

"I promise you I'll never do this again," I told the judge at the hearing. "I will never come back to your courtroom again if I get just one more chance."

He wasn't hearing it.

"Mr. Davis, I'm going to revoke one year of your probation."

All of those mixtapes. All the momentum I'd gotten back. It meant nothing. I was headed back to Rice Street.

XV

LEMON

The last time I was in Fulton County—before and after I got sent to the hole—I'd been placed in a segregated part of the jail because of my status as a known rapper. But it was full of snitches and people with high-profile cases, as mine was. My placement there was at the request of my attorneys, who were convinced someone trying to make a name for themselves would target me. And they were right; I'd been targeted.

Regardless of whether it was a smart precaution, being in there was a problem. It did not sit well with me that I was this gangster rapper talking about hitting licks and moving bricks in my music, but then I was hiding with rats when I got locked up. I wanted to be treated like everyone else. So when I returned to Fulton County in the fall of 2008, I signed a waiver to be in general population.

There were daily fights, stabbings, and even a shooting during that stint. But as vicious as that place was, I never had any issues there after the incisor incident in '05. For the most part I found that people respected me. Those who didn't knew better than to test me. It would not have been a good idea. I was already fuming over getting locked up on some bullshit. If anyone tried to approach or handle me in any type of way, it would not have been a move that would end in their favor. If anything, niggas were doing their best to stay out of my way.

I spent my time smoking weed, writing raps, and keeping in touch with the outside world on a cell phone I'd managed to get, minding my business until I could go home. But outside the walls of Fulton County, there was shady shit going on.

·

There was this song called "Make tha Trap Say Aye" that was on my mixtape *So Icey Boy*. That tape dropped in April, five months before I was sent back to prison. "Make tha Trap Say Aye" was a song I'd made in Zay's basement and gotten OJ on. It started to get a little buzz in the city over the summer.

Soon after I went to jail I started hearing the song made it to radio. This would have been great news if it weren't for the fact that people were calling it OJ's song. Originally, I'd had the first verse on it, but somehow now OJ did. I'd been moved to the second verse and OJ was closing things out with a new third verse. The whole dynamic of the song had changed. "Make tha Trap Say Aye" was now OJ da Juiceman featuring Gucci Mane.

The success of the song would land OJ a record deal at Asylum, which Deb facilitated. On the one hand I was happy for Juice. It wasn't like I needed "Make tha Trap Say Aye." I just didn't like that he and Deb had backdoored me.

That was some bullshit. I had gotten OJ hot. Fuck the song.

I promise you I didn't care about some song. I had several of 'em going. What I cared about was that I'd been the one taking OJ on the road with me, introducing him to different markets, helping him build a fan base. Juice had never even left Georgia before he joined me on tour. I was all for him getting his chance to blow, but when it happened, I felt like I should have been a part of it.

One of the people on the outside I kept in touch with was DJ Holiday. Holiday and I had done the *EA Sportscenter* tape together, and as my release date neared he and I got to talking about doing another one as soon as I got out.

Holiday wanted to do a mixtape called *Writing on the Wall*, which I thought was lame as hell. I was sure people would clown me for naming my shit after a Destiny's Child album. But Holiday had his mind set and he had a whole vision for the cover design.

"This is some jail shit!" he insisted. "It'll be hard as fuck, like you were in there carving these raps into the wall!"

He talked me into it. I wasn't thinking too hard about the title anyway. I had written hundreds of verses. I needed to get back into the studio and get things going again. Holiday told me I had songs that were killing the clubs, like "Bricks" and "Photo Shoot" and "Gucci Bandana" with Soulja Boy and Shawty Lo, but I still felt I'd wasted a lot of time being in jail.

Deb organized a homecoming party at Metronome Studios the night I got out. It was a big affair, with a whole bunch of important industry folks in attendance. The party was for everyone else, though. I was itching to work. As soon as Zay showed up I had him load up some beats to get the ball rolling.

A couple songs in, Zay waved me out of the booth. He had a request.

"Do something for me," he said. "When I play this next one

just go in. Don't even think about a hook and don't do any of those writtens. Let's see what comes out."

I had pages and pages of raps I'd written in jail, so those were the songs I started up with when I got back into the studio. I wanted to get them recorded so I could move on to new stuff. But I had no problem doing a freestyle for Zay. That was nothing. I liked an audience at the studio. A lot of rappers won't freestyle in a packed room, but I thrived on that type of pressure. It pushed me to go harder.

I stepped back into the booth and put the headphones on. Zay played the beat and I was off to the races.

I'm starting out my day with a blunt of purp
No pancakes, just a cup of syrup
Baking soda, pot, and a silver fork
You already know it's time to go to work

"Damn!!! That's it!!!"

As soon as I let those four bars off, my buddies outside the booth went crazy. I lost my momentum. I looked out the window to tell Zay to start the beat over, but he'd already gotten out of his chair.

"You know you're killin' this right now?" he said.

Killing what? I'd only rapped four bars. I wasn't sure what Zay was talking about, but he wasn't alone in his thinking. We'd already made a bunch of songs and nothing had gotten a reaction close to this. Zay started up the beat again and I regained my focus and finished the freestyle.

I'm back up in the kitchen workin' with a chicken
You get 63 grams for like $1,250

50 pounds of purp, 50 pounds of midget
As soon as it's gone I sell another 60
My baby need some shoes, my aunty need a purse
Summer coming real soon so I need a vert
I hop up out that van with that duffle bag
And if a nigga try me I'ma bust his ass
I'm countin' up money in my living room
Birds everywhere, I call it the chicken room
Pills in the cabinet, pounds in the den
Attic full of good, basement full of Benjamins
Two AK-47s and a blowtorch
Couple junkies knocking hard on my front porch
A couple old schools in my backyard
If I don't know ya I'ma serve you through my burglar bars
Gucci back bitch, yeah I'm back bitch
Did you miss me or miss my raps bitch?
This that new shit, that county jail shit
That seventh-floor Rice Street straight-out-a-cell shit
You on my shit list, I'm on the Forbes list
Since I'm a rich nigga, I need a rich bitch
I got a sick wrist, it cost 'bout six bricks
I'm on that slick shit, that Zone 6 shit

When I exited the booth every person in the studio had their eyes on me, looking bewildered. Zay had goose bumps. Holiday looked like he just watched me walk on water.

It was like I'd just spit the hardest shit these people had ever heard in their lives. I loved it. The song became "First Day Out."

Making that song is one of those moments I'll always remember. After what happened with "Make tha Trap Say Aye" while I was locked up things were feeling kind of funny between me and Deb, OJ, and even Zay. These were supposed to be my closest allies and I was unsure of where I stood with them anymore. The strain on those relationships went on for a while with Deb and Juice but when I made "First Day Out" with Zay, it reminded me this guy was my partner that I came in the game with. We were still here. I wasn't about to anything change that.

Later in the week I was back at Metronome working with Fatboi, and for some reason I kept thinking about this line I'd laid down the night before while I was working with Drumma Boy at Patchwerk. I was stuck on it.

Rock-star lifestyle, might don't make it, living life high every day clique wasted

"What you think about doing a song called 'Wasted'?" I finally asked Fatboi.

"Wasted? Hmm. Isn't that something white people say?"

Exactly.

I always found it funny when white people said they were getting "wasted" instead of drunk or fucked-up or whatever term that black folks used.

Fatboi saw the vision immediately. He ran with it. If we could take this suburban white slang and flip it and make it hood— that could be big. Then white America would pick it up and it'd bounce back into suburbia and we'd make this phrase hot again.

That line—*Rock-star lifestyle, might don't make it, living life high every day clique wasted*—had been part of a verse the other night, but maybe it could be the hook. I started rapping it to Fatboi and he got to making a beat. By the time he laid the ground-work for it and I made a verse to go with the hook, "Wasted" was sounding good.

I called up Plies, another artist I'd kept in touch with during my time in the county. I told him I wanted him on the song. He was all for it, so Fatboi sent him the track. Five minutes later my phone rang. It was Plies.

"Gucci, this is gon' be a number one," he told me. "I'm 'bout to do my verse and send it right back. Go record a third verse for it, okay?"

I laughed. "Wasted" was shaping up to be a cool song, but Plies and Fatboi were a little too much with all this talk of a number one smash hit. So Fatboi and I got to work on another song. Then Plies called again.

"You do the third verse yet?" he asked impatiently. "I thought I told you this shit is out of here!"

I did the third verse and went on with my life. "Wasted" was hard and I'd definitely put it on the *Writing on the Wall* tape with Holiday. Beyond that I wasn't thinking much about it.

Two months after I got out, I released *Writing on the Wall.* Two weeks after that I was performing at a club in Jacksonville, North Carolina, when the crowd started chanting for "Wasted."

"Wasted, Wasted, Wasted!"

I didn't even remember the lyrics to "Wasted." I hadn't recited it one time since the night I recorded it at Fatboi's studio. But Holiday had it on his laptop and when he played it the crowd went fucking crazy. I fumbled through the performance, trying to remember how the damn song went.

Fatboi and Plies were right. "Wasted" was something special. It was obvious this song was destined for bigger things than my mixtape. I had a lot of songs going in the clubs then, but "Wasted" was kind of like "Freaky Gurl" in how the masses took to it. What Fatboi and I talked about in the first five minutes of working on "Wasted," the concept of the song and what it would do, was exactly what had happened.

This had to be the lead single for my next album. Except I wasn't on great terms with my label and there weren't really plans for a next album. Ever since the dismal release of *Back to the Trap House,* I'd withdrawn from dealing with them. I'd just gone hard with the mixtapes. So I wasn't too hot on Asylum and I know a lot of people there weren't big on me either. *Back to the Trap House* was no moneymaker for them and the other thing was that at some point I'd dissed T.I., the biggest artist on Atlantic's roster. The label wasn't happy about that.

But "Wasted" required immediate attention. Plies and I had originally agreed to swap songs, but now that the record was booming he was asking for like forty thousand dollars for his verse. Negotiations between him and Deb went nowhere and a decision was made to remake "Wasted" without Plies and put Waka and OJ on it.

Waka and OJ both did hard verses but it just wasn't the same. I hadn't realized it at first but there was something about Plies's presence on the song . . .

I don't wear tight jeans like the white boys
But I do get wasted like the white boys

Something about that opening line too. Originally Plies's verse had started differently, with the backend part *Walked in the club, pocket full of big faces.* But Fatboi had moved the white-boys line to the beginning. It captured the essence of the song. Plies needed to be on this record.

The solution to that problem, as well as my issues at the label, came by way of my guy Todd Moscowitz. Todd had been promoted from president and CEO of Asylum to executive vice president of Warner Bros., a sister label of Atlantic. Todd had fought for me since day one and he was still fighting for me. He brought me over to Warner Bros. with him. Right away I started getting the support from the label I'd always wanted.

I now had my own imprint, 1017 Brick Squad, which I named after my childhood home in Bessemer. The formation of 1017 meant the dissolution of So Icey Entertainment, which meant the end of Deb's stake in my label. I was still rolling with Deb, but I was pleased she no longer owned a part of my label after the whole situation with OJ.

I made Waka my first sign to 1017 Brick Squad. Deb wasn't happy, but she couldn't do shit about it. She had to accept that one. Waka and I were inseparable and he was fiercely loyal. Even though it involved his momma, Waka knew what Deb and Juice did was a suspect move. He told me he would never do something like that. I knew he meant it. There was no way at that moment in time that Waka was signing to anyone but me. It just wasn't going to happen.

"Wasted" wasn't the only song I had making noise. Shortly after I came home I'd spent some time working with Sean Garrett, the songwriter and producer known for Usher's hit "Yeah!" Sean had this song he'd written for Mario, another R & B singer, called "Break Up" and he asked me to get on there. I did and after Greg Street from V-103 premiered the record on the radio a few weeks later, "Break Up" was outta here. Gone. I'd had hit records, but "Break Up" ended up being a pivotal crossover moment in my career.

Ever since what happened with "So Icy," I had a bad taste in my mouth when it came to collaborating with other artists. It wasn't something I did a lot of. *Hard to Kill* had some features from La Chat and Gangsta Boo, but those were exceptions to the rule. I'd just always been such a fan of Memphis rappers that it was special for me to get to work with them. The features on *Back to the Trap House* had been collaborations set up by the label.

And other artists weren't lining up to work with me either. I'd been blackballed in the industry. A year or so back I was supposed to be on Usher's song "Love in This Club," and then when I heard it on the radio I wasn't on there and Jeezy was. Incidents like that had kept me away from collaborating for a long time.

After "Break Up" the floodgates opened. There was Trey Songz's "LOL :)," Omarion's "I Get It In," Jamie Foxx's "Speak French," and a lot of others. Suddenly I was the go-to guy to get a verse from. Every song I touched was hitting the Billboard charts.

I knew I was something serious when I got the call that Mariah Carey wanted me on the remix to her song "Obsessed." This was beyond rap. This was pop.

I flew out to New York City to meet her, but when I got to the studio, Mariah wasn't there.

I was thinking that this was a waste of time. I could have easily done this from Atlanta. I was readying to leave after I finished my verse when the studio engineer told me to wait because Mariah wanted to hear the finished product. Then, out of nowhere she magically appeared, like she'd been there the whole time waiting for me to finish. I couldn't make sense of that, but the good news was she loved my verse. Not only that, she wanted my advice on some of the other songs she had for her upcoming album. She played me this Jermaine Dupri rework of an old hit out of Atlanta called "Swing My Way," which was originally by K.P. and Envyi.

"Who do you think I should get on this?" she asked me.

I told her put Juice on there. Mariah wasn't familiar with OJ but she valued my opinion and off my cosign he ended up on a Mariah Carey album. I got on it too, and then Jermaine Dupri got Big Boi from OutKast to do a verse for it. Coming all the way up to New York hadn't been a waste of time after all.

With "Wasted" on the rise and all these features on the airwaves, it was the perfect time to get an album out for Warner Bros. I'd decided to title it *The State vs. Radric Davis*.

This was when I reconnected with a former acquaintance, Coach K. Coach was working with a girl he brought to Deb with the hope that she could help get her career off the ground. Nicki Minaj had just put out *Beam Me Up Scotty* and Deb was getting a lot of credit for her success, so a lot of girls at the time were going to Deb thinking she could do something for them.

When I first saw Coach over at Deb's office, my attitude was *Fuck this guy.* He'd been on the other side of my war in 2005.

But Coach wasn't riding with that dude anymore. Something had gone down and they'd fallen out. Deb thought Coach could be an asset and he proved himself to be one when he lined up a batch of high-paying features for me. I was always down to make some money, so I dropped the grudge. More than that, Coach knew his shit when it came to the music game, much more so than Deb, who had always been more of a motherly figure to me than an experienced manager. The stakes had never been higher going into the making of *The State vs. Radric Davis*. I realized I needed the expertise of someone like Coach, so he and I began working together.

•

I was spending a lot of time in Las Vegas that summer. I'd always been a gambler. My father had been letting me in on his dice games since I was ten. Now that I had big money coming in, I was getting out to Vegas as often as possible. My game was craps and my spot was the Palms, where I stayed in the twenty-five-thousand-dollar-a-night Hugh Hefner Sky Villa, a two-story, nine-thousand-square-foot suite with an elevator and a glass-wall jacuzzi that overlooked the Las Vegas Strip. Downstairs was an eight-thousand-square-foot recording studio, so the place was like Disneyland to me.

During one of these trips Coach told me the producer Bangladesh was in town for UFC 100, which was supposedly the biggest UFC event ever. Bangladesh loved the UFC fights. He always talked about that shit. Bang was a year removed from the success of Lil Wayne's "A Milli." I wanted a crazy beat like that.

I was high as hell when I got up with Bang at the Palms' studio. It was one of those nights and I was only halfway into it. I was feeling super cocky, I told Bang to play me the beat that every other rapper had passed on. Something nobody else could handle. That would be a worthy challenge for me. Bang said he had something for me.

This beat was retarded and I went in right away, freestyling about lemonade and canary diamonds and a yellow Aston Martin. Lemonade-complexion east Australian girls. Everything yellow. The initial idea came from me running out of Sprite to pour my lean into that night and instead using lemonade.

Like with so many of my big records, I didn't know how big

"Lemonade" would be when I made it. Picking the winners was never easy considering how much I was recording. Truthfully, I was kind of distracted. I was in Vegas mode. My mind was on girls and gambling. I had a party going on in my room and was eager to get back to it. After I freestyled the verse and came up with a hook, I did just that.

When I popped back into the studio a few hours later, Bang had cooked up another beat for me to jump on: "Stupid Wild." Lil Wayne and Cam'ron eventually ended up on that one too.

I love the songs that came out of that session because they were made in the middle of one of my wild Vegas nights. Not before the party started. Not in the aftermath. During. You hear it in me. The energy of Sin City.

A week or two after I got back to Atlanta I got a call from Bang. We'd never gotten around to finishing "Lemonade." I'd actually forgotten about it. That whole weekend was a blur.

Bang hadn't. He'd been working on it.

"Look, I changed it around a little, but I think you're going to like it."

Bangladesh had swapped my hook for one that featured his daughter and little nieces singing.

Lemons on the chain with the V-Cuts
Lemons on the chain with the V-Cuts
Lemonade and shade with my feet up
Lemonade and shade with my feet up
Lemon pepper wings and a freeze cup
Lemon pepper wings and a freeze cup
Lemons in their face, watch 'em freeze up
Lemons in their face, watch 'em freeze up

Bangladesh had delivered. This new hook was better than what I'd done, and the finished beat for "Lemonade" was harder than what he had played me at the Palms.

•

Halfway into the making of *The State vs. Radric Davis* I violated my probation. I'd pissed dirty and left town without a permit. Those were the technicalities that triggered the violation, but really I was behaving badly all around. Of course at the time I didn't think I was doing anything wrong. I was just having a lot of fun spending this money. You ever see that movie *Get Him to the Greek*? It was something like that.

Once again the violation couldn't have happened at a worse time. Todd, Coach, and my lawyers sprung into action and hatched a plan to check me in to rehab. Their thinking was that the judge wouldn't pull me out of rehab and send me to jail if I was seeking treatment. I'd still have a court date when I got out for a probation violation hearing, but the chances of me not getting sent back to jail would be a whole lot better if I was fresh off a ninety-day drug treatment program. As far as contingency plans go, this one wasn't bad. But I didn't go easy.

Treatment was going to cost around fifty thousand dollars. While that wasn't breaking the bank, it was enough of an excuse for me to refuse. Plus ninety days of rehab meant ninety days of not doing shows or features, so there was real money at stake.

"Look, Todd, I got bills to pay," I told him.

"We'll cover the bills, Gucci," he told me. "Please, just go."

Todd talked me into it but when he met with Tom Whalley, the chairman and CEO of Warner Bros., he wouldn't put the money up. He said he'd only cut a check for two months of the three-month program. It had taken so much for Todd to get me to agree to go to rehab in the first place. He knew that if he came to me and said I'd have to pay out of my own pocket, it would be the last conversation he and I would have about rehab. But Todd did tell me about his meeting with Tom, and then he told me he was going to write me a personal check to cover the last month.

"So . . ." he said as he wrote out the check. "You know you've got to get this back to me at some point?"

I had *always* liked Todd. He had become a confidant and trusted adviser. Even when I met him 2004 and he had the Mohawk and I thought the dude was crazy, I liked the guy. But when he wrote me that personal check, that really meant something. That moment solidified us as friends on a deeper level.

I was still in complete denial about my drug problem. To me a drug addict was like the J's I'd served growing up in East Atlanta. Broke. Desperate. Missing teeth. That wasn't me. I was just enjoying an exciting lifestyle and it wasn't affecting my pockets. But I didn't want to let Todd and everyone else invested in my career down. So I went to rehab.

•

My time at the Talbott Recovery addiction treatment center was not unlike my time at Georgia Perimeter College. I was there but I wasn't really *there*. I didn't know what to expect when I checked in, but the place wasn't so bad. The folks there were mostly good people. But I was so bored. I'd been out having the time of my life, traveling from city to city, selling out shows, and now I had to sit in a circle with strangers and talk about problems I didn't believe

I had. I had committed to staying sober throughout rehab, but I couldn't wait to get it over with.

There was still a possibility I'd be sent to jail even after I completed rehab, so *The State vs. Radric Davis* needed to be ready to go. That meant I had to bend the rules. With the help of this cool white dude who worked at the center I began sneaking out in the middle of the night to record. He'd kindly cover me. At the time, the big thing in the industry was live-streaming studio sessions on Ustream, but I had to let producers I was working with know that I couldn't be on camera because I was supposed to be sound asleep at rehab.

Sober and with a hard deadline in front of me, I was more focused and determined than ever, and it resulted in some of my best music. I'd always thought I needed to be high to record, but I discovered I was making some of my best songs clean. I even put the freestyling on hold and got back to writing. Not just writing verses but writing full songs. Records like "Heavy," "Worst Enemy," even "Wasted," which was done before the rehab. I made all those songs sober.

Speaking of "Worst Enemy," I ran into him during my time at Talbott.

I'd been granted a two-day break to go home and see my family and friends. The idea was for me to get acquainted with living a sober life outside of rehab.

I was out to lunch at Houston's in the Lennox Mall. It was me, Coach, Polow, and the rapper Chubbie Baby. Jeezy and one of his boys happened to be there too, but I didn't see them until I left the restaurant. They were standing outside waiting for us.

This was a very, very weird situation. Jeezy had just dissed me and OJ on "24-23" after I sent a few shots his way on a track called "Hurry" off *Writing on the Wall*.

Jeezy and I hadn't looked each other in the eye in over four years. The only reason nothing popped off in the years since everything went down was that we hadn't seen each other.

For years people had kept us separate. We'd recently been booked on back-to-back shows—102 JAMZ's SuperJam in North Carolina and Hot 107.9's Birthday Bash in Atlanta—but the radio folks had me perform and then leave before Jeezy got there, and vice versa. No club would dare have us appear the same night. They knew some shit would go down. We were always positioned so that we weren't around each other. Now here we were. Face-to-face, standing outside of Houston's.

"What's up?" he asked.

"What's happening?" I responded.

Jeezy and Coach had unresolved issues of their own so they took a stroll, leaving me standing with Jeezy's boy. This nigga had a stupid look on his face like he was getting ready to do something. Polow told me he had my back and I laughed, assuring him I had my own back. Even though I was laughing, mentally I was bracing myself for an altercation.

A couple of minutes later Jeezy and Coach came back. Jeezy asked if he and I could talk. I agreed. We took a walk and then something strange happened—the tension wasn't there. There wasn't even a bad vibe between us.

"I wanted to chop it up," he told me. "Those young boys you're running with are causing trouble out here."

Here was the situation. Waka and his best friend, Slim Dunkin, had been getting into it with niggas in Jeezy's crew. This would all become public a year later when Waka and Jeezy's boy

Slick Pulla got to fighting at Walters Clothing and Dunk knocked out some other CTE guy at a flea market, but all of that had been brewing for a while. None of this had anything to do with me. This was Waka and Dunk being young and crazy.

"I think we should get the young boys to chill," Jeezy suggested. "Ain't nobody gonna get hurt but one of them."

He had a point. I was in rehab and Jeezy wasn't in the streets anymore. If anyone was going to get hurt, it was going to be one of them and I didn't want anything happening to Waka or Dunk.

"You're right," I told him. "I can talk to them."

I realized in that moment that Jeezy knew he had blood on his hands from everything that had happened. Now he was trying to prevent another bad situation from happening. I couldn't argue with that. I agreed with it. Jeezy didn't know this but I'd just made "My Worst Enemy." On that track I more or less said I was ready to move on from all my beefs. So it was a crazy coincidence that we were sitting here looking to do what I'd written about in that unreleased song.

We met again the next day. We sat down, agreed to a truce, and said we'd put our history behind us. We even agreed to work on music. Jeezy had just done a song with Zay called "Trap or Die 2." That was a problem for me when I heard about it. I didn't like Zay working with Jeezy but the song was so hard. After we established the truce, Jeezy told me to hop on the remix. At the same time I'd just made "Heavy," which was produced by Shawty Redd, and I told Jeezy he should get on there with me. We both had these songs with each other's go-to producers and now we were going to swap. This would be a moment people would care about. Our beef had affected so many more people than just us over the years. This would unite the city.

•

Toward the end of my stay at Talbott I was granted another two-day break and I needed it. It was crunch time for my album and there was work to be done.

I had an unfinished record called "Bad Bad Bad." This was a song Fatboi produced and we were waiting on a feature from Keyshia Cole, who had already signed up to sing the hook.

Coach and I booked a flight to Houston to meet up with Keyshia and finish "Bad Bad Bad." Talbott didn't permit travel so this was a risky move, but it was one I felt I had to make.

Coach and I boarded a flight to Houston. We were forty-five minutes from our destination when the boom of thunder shook us out of our seats. Moments later the strike of lightning pierced the black sky. That's when I saw it: a tornado ripping its way through the night. The plane shook as the pilot announced that we were flying through a severe storm. We were told to brace for turbulence.

I turned around to find passengers in prayer, flight attendants included. The storm bellowed as I heard muted crying. I looked at Coach. We didn't exchange any words but I knew we were thinking the same thing. Maybe this was it. We bowed our heads and all I could think of was my son.

I know what you're thinking. What son? Truth is I didn't know him all that well either. I'd only learned I had a child a year before. He was already ten months old. A girl I used to see had a baby and people were saying it looked like me. I hadn't even known she was pregnant. I reached out and asked her if it was mine. She was unsure. I took a blood test and sure enough, I was the father of a little boy.

The circumstances under which I'd learned I was a father

weren't ideal—almost a year after his birth, to a woman I wasn't in a relationship with or in love with. Still, I was happy. I'd always loved children.

I hadn't been able to embrace my new role as a father. Between getting sent back to jail, my career being busier than ever, and the drugs, I hadn't been in my son's life as much as I should have. But in that moment, with the plane shaking, he was all I could think about.

The storm wasn't letting up but I found peace knowing that if this was it, I wouldn't be leaving my boy empty-handed. I'd made enough to give him a start, enough to give him a chance to follow whatever it was he wanted to do with his life, without having to take the same risks that his father did.

With clenched fists, we were relieved to hear we'd soon make an emergency landing in Houston. But this airport only housed American Airlines. Our Delta flight couldn't deplane here. The pilot announced we were to wait until the storm passed, at which point he'd bring us to our original destination. How long that would take, he didn't know. For me time was of the essence. Coach and I demanded to be let off the plane. After an argument with the crew, they gave in. We exited out of the rear of the plane, where we took a car service to the studio to wrap up "Bad Bad Bad" with Keyshia.

I kept the whole story of our flight a secret after we returned to Atlanta the next day. I could have been rearrested for traveling without a permit. Even though I'd never speak about it again, the dramatic experience stuck with me. I really thought it was over.

•

My time at Talbott was nearing an end, but I needed the staff there to do me one last favor. The BET Hip Hop Awards were approaching and I was being given the opportunity to perform three times that night. I'd do "Pretty Girls" with Wale, "Gucci Bandana" with Soulja Boy and Shawty Lo, and then I'd have my own set where I'd bring out Plies for "Wasted" and Mario for "Break Up." This was a big look. I needed to attend this.

"This is my career," I explained. "I have to be there."

As they'd been throughout the ninety-day program, the staff at Talbott was accommodating and cool, especially after I told them I would record a public service announcement that would air during the broadcast. Not only would this get me the green light to attend, but it would be an asset when I appeared in front of the judge, a court date that was now looming.

"Yo, it's ya boy Gucci. I want y'all to know that I do make party records and it's all fun, but on a serious note I'm taking my own sobriety very seriously and it's for real. That's coming from ya boy Gucci. Be safe."

Truthfully I hadn't absorbed much of what they'd been teaching me at Talbott. I'd gone to rehab to avoid going to jail and I wasn't leaving a changed man. I was excited to have some fun again. But I did feel good about my time there. Aside from the late-night excursions, I'd held up my end of the bargain and stayed sober the whole time. And I'd made a great album. I deserved to have that moment at the BET Hip Hop Awards. And what a moment it was.

My last covert escape out of Talbott had been a trip to the airport, where I'd met my jeweler. I had him design all this jewelry for me that I wanted to unveil at the award show. The canary diamonds Arm & Hammer baking soda box chain, the Atlanta Falcons helmet chain, the Atlanta Hawks jersey chain, the big Brick Squad circle chain, the square Brick Squad chain, the iced-out whisk chain—we're talking hundreds of thousands of dollars' worth of jewelry, and that was just the chains. We won't even get into the bracelets, watches, or pinky rings. Talbott had sent a chaperone to accompany me to the event and she couldn't believe it when she saw me putting it all on. Where had all this stuff been? I'd kept it hidden in my backpack ever since my rendezvous with my jeweler.

But the 2009 BET Hip Hop Awards was more than an opportunity to stunt. It was a culmination and validation of years of hard work I'd put in. *Trap House*'s success had been marred by the murder charge. *Back to the Trap House* had flopped. I had to go to jail right as my mixtape run began to pay off. But I'd kept at it. I'd stayed persistent and now I was here. One month away from the release of *The State vs. Radric Davis*. This album would be the one. I knew it. Every time I hit the stage that night I could feel my impact in the Atlanta Civic Center. It wasn't the pyrotechnics. It was me.

And these folks cheering me on didn't even know what I had planned. I'd just dropped *The Burrprint* mixtape with Drama a day before and I was about to drop three mixtapes at once the following week. *The Cold War* series. *Guccimerica* with DJ Drama, *Great Brrritain* with DJ Scream, and *BRRRUSSIA* with DJ Holiday. I felt unstoppable.

A month later I checked out of Talbott after completing the program in full. The next day a judge sentenced me to serve another year in Fulton County Jail.

XVI

BALL TILL YA FALL

I started smoking weed again immediately after being sent back to Fulton County. I was livid. I'd gone to rehab. I'd done that corny PSA. I couldn't believe it was all for nothing. What a waste of my time. This was even worse than when they sent me to jail over the community service bullshit.

To make matters worse, the "truce" with Jeezy proved to be short-lived. I should have known better. Our plan to swap songs fell apart after I got locked up. Jeezy never did his verse for "Heavy" and Warner Bros. moved forward promoting the song without him. Jeezy had sent me the files for "Trap or Die 2," but when I recorded a verse and put it out, he tried to act like it wasn't a real collaboration. He pitched it like I'd just taken it upon myself to remix his song.

In December 2009, right before *The State vs. Radric Davis* came out, DJ Drama had me call into his Hot 107.9 radio show from jail when Jeezy was in the studio. Drama set it up as if Jeezy and I were just now speaking for the first time in years, but that shit was so fake. The conversation was chopped up and edited and the whole thing sounded forced. The only reason I did it was that I was looking to find a way to drum up excitement for my album from behind bars. The reality was that Jeezy and I had already made up and fallen out again over the songs before that call happened.

I'm getting a little ahead of myself, but I saw Jeezy at a club after that stint in Fulton County. I knew the situation with the songs hadn't worked out, but I still thought we reached an understanding that our beef was behind us. So I said what up. He was so uncomfortable seeing me.

"We just can't do it right here in front of everybody," he whispered. "Not right now."

In a way I understood it. Jeezy was in the club with twenty of his goons. I imagine he'd probably been saying "Fuck Gucci" for so many years that he didn't want to appear cool with me in front of them. A chump move, but I got it. That was the last time Jeezy and I ever spoke.

Still, I respected that he sat down with me at Houston's that day. Man-to-man. One-on-one. To be honest I never thought he'd have the guts to face me like that.

•

The State vs. Radric Davis was the success we'd hoped for. I'd finally hit the sweet spot: a project that was that next level—bigger than the mixtapes—but still me. It had the A-list features— Usher, Wayne, Cam'ron, Mike Epps—on the interludes, but it still had my core four horsemen—Zay, Shawty Redd, Fatboi, and Drumma Boy—producing the bulk of the beats.

"His second official album differentiates itself with excellent production, especially the rumbling beats of Bangladesh and Drumma Boy, and with guests such as Lil Wayne and Usher. But the star is Gucci, with his deep grab bag of rhymes that aim at funny bones. It's a winning combination: a heavy ego and a light touch."

—*Rolling Stone*

"*The State vs. Radric Davis* has proved the rapper's case beyond a reasonable doubt. So when rap fans ask if he is now a bankable hip-hop star, let the record show that Gucci Mane is guilty as charged."   —*XXL*

"The LP has an energy rare to major-label rap efforts. Like Wayne's *Tha Carter II*, it translates Gucci's mixtape triumphs into something more digestible and immediate."   —*Pitchfork*

Despite the piss-poor timing of getting locked up right before my album's release, we were prepared for that scenario. We'd already shot music videos with director Mr. Boomtown for "Lemonade," "Heavy," "I Think I Love Her," "Photoshoot," "Bingo," "Wasted," and "Worst Enemy." Those were in the bank and ready to roll out at our convenience. *XXL* wanted me on the cover of their February issue. A year earlier I'd been on there alongside OJ, Shawty Lo, and Soulja Boy, but this time around they were giving me my first solo cover. Behind bars or not, I was the shit.

There was one thing I hadn't planned for: my newfound popularity with these white hipster kids. Todd had been telling me

I had this alternative fan base. "Lemonade" had especially connected with them. My songs were getting remixed by EDM DJs who played huge music festivals around the world.

I liked EDM. The big beats, the lights at the shows, the way the crowd responded. It was a world away from the hood-ass clubs in Decatur I was used to, but I liked that my music was touching different audiences. That was cool to me.

One of the DJs who was championing my music was Diplo. Apparently he was big in this scene. He'd been nominated for a Grammy for his work on M.I.A.'s song "Paper Planes." Hoping to further solidify my place in this world, Todd and Coach sent Diplo my a capellas from the *Cold War* tapes. He recruited a whole gang of DJs and made *Free Gucci*, a mixtape with EDM remixes of the best songs from the trilogy. It took off.

Meanwhile, my shooter-turned-rapper and right-hand man Waka had stepped up in my absence and made a name for himself just like OJ had a year prior. Only this time Waka was carrying the torch for 1017. I'd given Waka his rap name, Waka Flocka Flame, and he took after me by going hard with the mixtapes. But Waka got himself hot with his own sound, his own songs, and his own crew of producers. It wasn't like what happened with "Make tha Trap Say Aye." "O Let's Do It" kicked everything off for Waka. He followed that up with "Hard in Da Paint." I couldn't have been prouder of him. The boy was going in.

After serving six months of my one-year sentence I was released from Fulton County. It was shortly after midnight, May 12, 2010. Outside I was greeted by friends, family, fans, and the media. I approached the reporters with Duke, Holiday, Shawty Lo, and Todd and read a statement.

First and foremost, I would like to thank my legal counsel, Dwight Thomas and Michael Holmes, for the excellent representation, as well as my label Asylum and Warner Bros. Records for sticking with me through my situation and helping me through my time behind bars.

Most importantly, I want to thank all of my fans for their support while I have been away. Your letters and words of encouragement helped me make it through. None of my success would be possible without you.

I have made some mistakes in my life and have hurt a lot of people who care about me. I will work very hard to get past that. Those mistakes have brought me to where I'm at today and they will not be repeated. These past few months have been a difficult time, but fortunately I have learned a great deal from my experience. I was able to do a great deal of soul-searching. I'm coming out with a new attitude toward life.

Unfortunately, my incarceration came at a pivotal part of my career. Just as my first major-label album was dropping I was forced to miss what should have been one of the proudest moments of my life. This is something I will make sure never happens again. My time in jail was trying, but I grew from it and am now stronger and a better person. I want to continue on a positive track and truly focus on being a role model to my fans and to my community. I'm looking toward the future with a newfound respect and appreciation for the law and a strong dedication to my music and career. With that in mind, I have already begun to make positive strides toward the future. I have launched a new label, 1017 Brick Squad Records, in affiliation with Asylum/Warner

THE AUTOBIOGRAPHY OF GUCCI MANE

Bros. Records and I'm working with a new team. I'm looking forward to getting back to business and start making hits. I am extremely excited about my new album, The Appeal, which will be dropping at the end of the summer.

Over the course of 2010, 1017 Brick Squad Records will be releasing albums from my artist Waka Flocka Flame, as well as my group Brick Squad, which features Waka, OJ da Juiceman, and myself. In July we'll be heading out on a nationwide tour, hitting venues around the country and continuing the movement.

Finally, a lot of things happened while I was away. I'm back to address these things. The rap game is in need of substance right now, and I'm here for the streets right on time. I can't wait to show the world why I feel that now that I'm free, ironically, I'm the most-wanted man in Georgia. I'm hungry for success and ready to compete, so may the competition begin. I set out five years ago to be the number one rapper in hip-hop and today that journey continues, with an even sharper focus. I challenge all artists to put out the best music they ever made this summer. I will accept nothing less than victory and I still want worthy opponents. So everyone who was there for me, thanks for y'all's support. Holla.

Of that entire statement, only the last part spoke to where my mind was at when I walked out of jail that night. The humble talk was for the lawyers, the cameras, Todd, whomever. In reality I was feeling myself more than ever. I was keenly aware of how my career and the artists signed to me had only grown stronger during my time away. "A newfound respect and appreciation for the law"? Give me a break. I was the hottest thing smokin'. No one could tell me shit anymore.

•

I kept up my usual routine: straight from jail to the studio. After a welcome-home dinner I was back at Patchwerk, where Drumma Boy had a batch of beats on a thumb drive waiting for me. He loaded them up. Two beats in and it was back to business. I stepped in the booth and proceeded to freestyle "Normal."

Hit the mall, spend 30 like that shit normal
Me and my broad nothin' but Gucci, Louis, Ferragamo
Drop racks, get it back
Call the shit Karma
Fuck models when I want
All your hoes normal
Blowin' Kush
What you smokin' smellin' really normal
Ask me if I wanna hit it
I don't really wanna
Pulled up, old school, paint Willy Wonka
Guts all white, but the rims abnormal
Backseat of my Rolls in my silk pajamas
Hoppin' out in house shoes like the shit normal
Change my jewelry every day, 'cause it's the summer
If yo bitch want my number
Chill it's really normal

The reaction to "Normal" in the studio was like when I did "First Day Out." I hadn't lost a step.

As I was knocking out the second verse to "Normal," Drumma Boy went over to Patchwerk's Studio B to work with Waka. That's when they made "No Hands" with Wale and Roscoe Dash, a record that would surpass the heights of "O Let's Do It" and "Hard in Da Paint" and take Waka from up-and-coming prospect to outright star. The song was such an obvious smash that as soon as they finished recording it there was a dispute over ownership. Folks from Interscope were at Patchwerk with Roscoe and they wanted to snatch it for his album. Lucky for Waka, Todd was there too, and he got back to his roots as a lawyer and won the power struggle. I wasn't there for any of that. I was still in Studio A, chewing up Drumma's beats.

The next day I got back up with Boomtown to kick off another run of music video shoots.

Back in March, while I was still locked up, my team released a mixtape called *Burrrprint (2)* for sale on iTunes, made up mostly of songs I'd made with Drumma Boy prior to getting locked up. That project sold like twenty thousand copies in its first week with little promotion, and a few of the joints off it had taken off. So I'd made sure Boomtown was ready to shoot videos as soon as I got home. We had five on deck. I already had the perfect video vixen lined up.

Keyshia Dior. I'd first seen her in Timbaland and Drake's "Say Something" video not long after I went back to Fulton County. Then I came across her again in *XXL*'s Eye Candy. She was the new chick in the industry and I had to meet her. I had my assistant Amina book her as soon as we locked in the dates with Boomtown.

The first video we shot was for "Everybody Lookin." The next day I had a photo shoot for *Rolling Stone* and then another video for "Boy from the Block." Keyshia wasn't scheduled to show up until the next day. We were going to shoot a video for "911 Emergency" at Club Life, but I caught word that she had gotten into town a day early. So I told Amina to bring her out to the set of "Boy from the Block."

The magazine photos didn't do her justice.

"You're gorgeous," I told her. There was no playing it cool.

"Thanks." She laughed. I must not have been the first one to tell her that.

I told Keyshia to stick around after we finished shooting "Boy from the Block" but she turned me down, telling me she'd see me the next day for our scheduled shoot. That only made me want her more.

We had such a good time on the set of "911 Emergency" the next day. Amina had hired a whole gang of models for that video but I made sure Keyshia knew she was my leading lady, that she had everything she needed in her dressing room, that she felt comfortable and taken care of. I wanted her to feel good about coming out here.

After we wrapped up I practically begged her to stay an extra night in Atlanta so I could take her to dinner. I'd done nothing but work since I got out of jail and this seemed like a break worth taking. She agreed.

Keyshia and I went to dinner at the InterContinental Hotel in Buckhead. We were still wearing our all-white matching outfits from the shoot. We ordered the same thing, salmon with mashed potatoes. I took her hand as we left the restaurant. The whole situation was out of character for me. I knew she was special.

Keyshia was stunning but it was more than that. I'd been with a lot of pretty girls. There was more to her. I may have first fell for her beauty, ogling her pictures while I was sitting in the clink, but I quickly began to appreciate her as a person.

Keyshia was from Jamaica. When she was ten her father was killed, and after that her mother moved her and her brothers out of the country. They spent a year in Canada before settling down in Miami.

After high school she enrolled in nursing college, following in the footsteps of her mother, a nurse practitioner. But Keyshia wasn't meant to be wearing scrubs. This was a girl who'd been voted best dressed in her class every year in high school. Her passion in life was clothes, makeup, and hair. Fashion and beauty. So she dropped out and enrolled in cosmetology school with a dream of becoming a stylist to the stars.

On a chance encounter Keyshia had gotten cast in that "Say Something" video and became something of a star herself. The girl was a fox with a look all her own. The chick with the Mohawk and blue lipstick.

She hadn't let the sudden success get the better of her. From the modeling jobs and paid appearances at nightclubs Keyshia had made herself some money in a few short months, but she'd saved it, she told me. She wanted to launch a line of cosmetics—lipstick, lip gloss, eye shadow, shit like that. As I watched her talk about her vision I could tell this wasn't somebody flapping her gums. This was someone who when she set out to do something, she did it.

We'd both been through a lot. A few years after the death of her father, one of her brothers got killed in an incident where a gun misfired. But Keyshia was like me. She was resilient. She was a survivor. I was so drawn to that.

We had our differences. Keyshia was not much of a partier and definitely didn't do drugs. She said she hardly even went out unless she was getting paid for an appearance. So I downplayed my vices. I'd already thought about what she may have heard about me or read online, so I didn't need to add any concerns. Plus I'd just gotten out of jail, so besides smoking weed I really hadn't done much partying or drugging of late.

We fell hard and fast for each other. Keyshia went home to Miami the next day but soon I asked her to join me on the road as I did my best to keep up with a grueling schedule of shows, media, and studio sessions. I was really into Keyshia but I was also very preoccupied with my career. I'd never been busier.

•

The State vs. Radric Davis had sold just short of a half million copies and Todd and Lyor had their sights set on my next album being an even bigger success. So did I. *Georgia's Most Wanted: The Appeal* would dwarf *The State vs. Radric Davis*. It was a foregone conclusion. My first night out I'd told the world that I was on a mission to become the biggest rapper in the world and I'd meant it.

I had to go even bigger with this album. I wanted to work with Swizz Beatz. Done. I wanted to work with Wyclef Jean. Not a problem. I wanted to work with Pharrell. Let's fly to California. Everything I wanted, Warner Bros. would accommodate. I was the priority.

And I was enjoying it. There's a line on that album—*I spent my winter in a jail so I'm ballin' all summer*—and that's what it was. I was making up for lost time. I'd always been a spender, but I took it up a notch that summer for real. I might walk into Magic

City on a weekday, throw twenty thousand dollars in the air, and leave thinking nothing of it.

I was about to appear on VH1's 2010 Hip Hop Honors show, where I was going to perform a cover of Master P's classic "I Miss My Homies." I was excited for that. P had been one of my biggest influences. I figured what better way to pay tribute to the original Ice Cream Man himself than to show up onstage with a three-hundred-thousand-dollar ice cream cone chain around my neck. Excessive? Not to me. Compared to all my chains with the crazy fruity colors, this was toning it down.

I got two Ferraris back to back. First was the black 612 Scaglietti. It was Memorial Day weekend and I was in Miami. I was doing an interview at DJ Khaled's radio station when they brought it to me. I walked outside and there it was, waiting for me on the tow truck. I wrote the man a check, they pulled that motherfucker off the trailer, and I hopped in and sped off. I remember my buddies were standing there in shock. I hadn't told anyone I was getting it.

When I got back to Atlanta I copped the yellow 458 Italia. I was the first person in the States to get that car. I put it on twenty-two-inch Forgiatos and had the interior customized with yellow stitching. The two new pets cost me a quick seven hundred grand.

I loved the W Hotel in South Beach, and me and my boys would go down there and turn up. I'd be in the Mega Ocean View Suite. It had its own basketball court. We'd be out there wagering a hundred dollars a shot. The suite had a shower in the center. I'd be in the bed with two girls while I watched two other girls shower together.

During one of those Miami trips we had to cut the party

short. A hurricane was coming so I chartered a jet to Atlanta. Once we were airborne I got up and went to the bathroom, rolled me a couple of blunts, and smoked 'em back to back.

When we touched down the pilot came out of the cockpit and he went crazy. He was so pissed. Unless I coughed up ten thousand dollars to clean the jet, he was calling the cops.

I paid the money and went on my way, but I couldn't believe I was paying ten extra bands for a damn blunt. I hadn't been trying to mess with the pilot. I just figured I'd be allowed to smoke, having spent this kind of money on a private flight. It hadn't even occurred to me I was doing something wrong.

I was spending money like it was never going to stop coming. Why would it? Some nights I was making ninety thousand dollars. I was pulling in sixty thousand at these stadium shows, like Hot 97's Summer Jam or Hot 107.9's Birthday Bash, and then I'd do an after-party and bring in another thirty thousand. I had songs all over the radio. The royalty checks were flowing. It never occurred to me that any of this could be temporary.

And then "Gucci Time" leaked.

"Gucci Time" was one of two songs that I'd made with Swizz Beatz for *The Appeal*. I liked it—I still like it—but I'd never considered it as the lead single for my album. I thought the other song I did with Swizz, "It's Alive," was better, plus I had this dope-ass record called "Haterade" I'd made with Pharrell and Nicki Minaj at Chalice Studios in Los Angeles. I couldn't wait for people to hear that one.

But Warner Bros. had been big on "Gucci Time" from the jump. They hired Chris Robinson to direct the music video. This was a Grammy-nominated director. His CV was iconic: Nas's "One Mic," Alicia Keys's "Fallin'," Jay-Z and Beyoncé's " '03 Bonnie & Clyde." I think Warner Bros. paid like two hundred thousand for the "Gucci Time" video.

When the song leaked they felt like they needed to move on it. The plans changed overnight and "Gucci Time" was positioned as the first single for *The Appeal*. It didn't work.

> "'Gucci Time' is banal, a rehash of Jay-Z's 'On to the
> Next One' with an unnecessarily shrill Justice sample.
> (Someone at Gucci HQ still hasn't figured out that it was
> the artist's untainted appeal, cf. 'Wasted' and 'Lemonade,'
> that made for his greatest commercial successes.)"
> —*Pitchfork*

> "The awfully ugly sounds he puts in for the synths are
> just terrible on the ears, though, and when Swizz comes
> in for his token verse about nothing, you realize how
> hard this song would be to listen to without Gucci on
> top of it." —*Pop Matters*

> "The problem is that the leaked songs were 'Gucci Time'
> and 'Weirdo,' which both seemed like recycled themes
> (i.e. T.I.'s 'Bring 'Em Out' = 'Gucci Time')" —*iHipHop*

That was what everyone was saying. Swizz's beat was a throwaway and I shouldn't be making that type of record to begin with.

I never really paid much mind to what critics said, but for some reason this response threw me for a loop. I didn't think "Gucci Time" should be the single, but I did like the song. It never crossed my mind that the response would be negative. For so long it seemed like every song I made was outta here. I was used to songs I hadn't thought twice about blowing up, so when the inverse happened I didn't handle it well. I wasn't prepared for that.

The Appeal was finished and turned in to Warner Bros. but the album's release was still a couple of months away and there was work to be done to promote it. But I started to withdraw from that work. I started bailing on photo shoots and interviews. A fan would ask me for an autograph and I would tell them to step off. Todd and I were still talking but I became disengaged. Keyshia and I broke up. Worst of all, I started drinking lean again. Heavily.

It had been almost a year since I'd touched the stuff. I'd spent those three months in rehab, immediately followed by six months in jail, and when I got out, I steered clear of it. But as time went on I convinced myself that I could handle it. I was working so hard and this was my way of taking the edge off.

Except I couldn't handle it. My tolerance was so low that when I started up drinking pints like I used to, it took a toll on my body. I was already spreading myself thin. The shows, the features, the videos, the interviews, my album. It was impossible to keep up after I reintroduced the drugs to my body. I needed to be focused and on point like I'd been before *The State vs. Radric Davis* came out. Instead I was self-sabotaging.

Looking back, I realize it was so unnecessary. The response to "Gucci Time" wasn't as bad as I made it out to be. There was no reason *The Appeal* couldn't have been a success. I'd felt good about that album. Really good. As far as the big picture, I was still a star. But I lost sight of the big picture. I couldn't see it. I was in too dark of a place.

This was how these downward spirals in my life always went. Some stressful situation would arise and I would turn to the drugs to cope. Abusing the lean and weed and pills would end up with me sleeping and eating poorly. It would compromise my whole health and then I wouldn't be on point to handle the original stressful situation right. I'd compound bad choices. That would lead to more problems, more stress, and more drugs. A cycle with no end. No good one at least.

After what happened in '05 and all my scuffles in the streets, I already had serious issues with paranoia. I would use the drugs to numb those feelings but really they magnified them. People have called me bipolar or that I suffer from depression, but I always identified most with the symptoms of someone with PTSD. Like a soldier who came home still dealing with the effects of being in a war zone.

It would always be a domino effect, with each fallen domino sending me deeper and deeper into despair until I crashed,

That Waka and I were having problems didn't help. Things between him and I had been rocky ever since I officially got rid of Deb as my manager earlier that year. She and my booking agent had gotten themselves, and by extension me, in big trouble after I missed a bunch of show dates due to being in rehab in '09.

The promoters never got their deposits back. I still had love for Deb and that whole family. We'd all been through a lot together. But there were too many problems going on with her as my manager. I was at a point in my career where I couldn't be involved.

But Deb had already been fired as Nicki's manager. So when I did the same, she was in a tough spot. This was her livelihood. Waka was always his own man, but even if he thought his momma was in the wrong, she was still his momma. He was stuck in the middle of a no-win situation. I knew that family very well, so I knew what kinds of things were being said about me in their house. Things were going to get tense.

Meanwhile "No Hands" was blowing up and Waka was outgrowing his role as my right-hand man. Everything was different now.

Two weeks before *The Appeal*'s release, I was in Los Angeles, getting ready to walk the red carpet of the MTV Video Music Awards. I was not in a good state of mind. I was becoming more reclusive, combative, paranoid, and isolated. The day before, Todd had called me to discuss a music video and I'd told him never to call me during the daytime again. That he was only allowed to call me after dark. Otherwise, I said, he and I were going to have a serious problem.

Outside the VMAs I was with Todd, Waka, Master P, and Joie Manda, the head of urban music at Warner Bros. Really I was alone in my own world. Dressed in black from head to toe, bloodshot eyes behind my sunglasses, I stood in silence, staring blankly into the distance.

This would happen from time to time, whenever my benders would reach their tipping point and manifest in the form of bizarre behavior and volatile outbursts. Spells where I would zone out and gaze into space. Sometimes I'd be looking into the mirror, mumbling to myself, trying to make sense of thoughts that didn't make any sense. Doctors had tried to give me medication for this before. Mood stabilizers. But I rarely took them. They made me even more sluggish. They zapped me of my energy, my creativity, my whole mojo.

I returned to reality, if only momentarily, when a staff member informed us we would require extra security before we could enter. Moments later ten LAPD officers showed up and proceeded to debate whether I was allowed in the venue.

I'd seen other celebrities arrive and walk in without a problem. Why was this happening to me? Why the fuck would these people invite me here and then do this to me? I grew increasingly agitated.

It was too little, too late by the time we were allowed to enter the Nokia Theatre. The flash of cameras from the media only angered me more. It felt like they were taunting me. I pulled out the ten-thousand-dollar stack in my pocket and threw it in their faces.

> "Feathers and glitter weren't the only things flying around the white carpet; Gucci Mane made his very own contribution by tossing out money—and lots of it. 'It was during the commercial break. He was on the photography press line and all of a sudden he whipped out a spot of cash, it was quite a bit,' said producer Matt Harper, who was standing at the top of the carpet. 'At first he was just sort of showing it to the cameras, and then all of a sudden he just sort of threw it and then there was chaos,' he continued." —MTV News (September 20, 2010)

I kept replaying the incident in my head during my flight back to Atlanta the next day. Me standing there on the white carpet of the VMAs, watching reporters fight over hundred-dollar bills like I was feeding pigeons.

That was so stupid. Why the fuck would I do that?

By the time the BET Hip Hop Awards rolled around in October, I was a shell of my former self. The release of *The Appeal* had come and gone. First-week sales weren't even bad. It sold sixty thousand copies. But it was nowhere near expectations. That was all my fault. I'd disappeared on the label after they gave me everything I wanted. This wasn't like when *Back to the Trap House* bombed. Then I could blame Asylum for putting out an album that misrepresented me as an artist. This was the album I'd wanted to make, and I dropped the ball.

I shouldn't have checked out after "Gucci Time" leaked. I shouldn't have put out the *Buy My Album* mixtape with Holiday a week before the album came out without telling anyone. Despite its title that took the attention away from my album. I shouldn't have bailed on the *SPIN* magazine photo shoot and ended the interview with their writer. My favorite song from *The Appeal*, "Making Love to the Money," had been popping off organically in the clubs, but I went and shot an X-rated video for it at Magic City. It couldn't be shown anywhere beyond WorldStarHipHop Uncut. I'd made a series of bad decisions. My whole strategy was fucked. There hadn't even been a strategy.

As I stepped onstage to perform "Gucci Time" at the BET Hip Hop Awards, I looked out into the crowd and remembered how it had been just a year before. I'd been sober, laser-focused, a month away from the release of *The State vs. Radric Davis*. I could see the difference in the crowd now. People weren't fucking with Gucci Mane like they had been then. Everything was slipping away from me.

XVII

LOST IN THE SAUCE

Things only got worse from there. A lot worse.

After the awards I went to Miami Beach, where I holed up in my condo on Allison Island. I arrived with nothing more than $150,000 in cash and my security guard Big Dame, who stood by while I tore it up for a week straight. I didn't leave the place once. Everything I needed—girls, drugs, drank—was brought to me. It was the type of bender rock stars were known for, not rappers.

My phone was blowing up with calls from Coach, Todd, and others concerned for my well-being. But I couldn't be reasoned with. I'd answer, cuss 'em out, hang up, and get back to whatever vice I happened to be indulging in at that moment.

After a week of this an intervention was planned to put an end to the madness. Dame explained that I'd been booked for a last-minute show in Vegas and that they'd chartered a jet to fly me there. Even in the midst of my tailspin, I was still down to make some money, especially if it meant going to Vegas, where I knew I could keep the party going.

Dame got me all the way back to Atlanta believing that. I was in such rough shape that even when we landed it didn't occur to me we'd only been in the air for two hours, less than half the time it takes to get to Vegas from Miami. It wasn't until we left the airport that I looked around and realized where I was. This was not Vegas. This was home, the last place I wanted to be.

I flipped out, attacking Dame in the van as we made the fifteen-minute drive to Riverwoods Behavioral Health System in Riverdale. Coach, my lawyer, and other members of my inner circle were waiting for me, begging me to check myself in to rehab.

The only one I paid the slightest attention to was my lawyer, who was telling me I'd failed *another* drug test and if I didn't check myself in, I'd almost certainly be sent to jail. After more than an hour of arguing outside Riverwoods, I relented, agreeing to a monthlong stay.

But that shit didn't last. I wasn't at the facility a week when I changed my mind and got a buddy to come sign me out. I'd realized I'd already fallen for my lawyer's line before. I wasn't doing rehab just so I could get out and get sent right to jail again. The couple of days at the Riverwoods center did little to slow me down. If anything, they were a brief pit stop on my road to total self-destruction. Two weeks after the failed intervention I reached the end of that road at an auto-body shop on Northside Drive.

I'd gotten it into my head that this guy who worked on my cars had played me out of some money. This wasn't just some mechanic. This was a friend of mine, someone who had joined me on the road before. But in my paranoid state, I convinced myself otherwise. I hopped into my Hummer and hit the gas, flying down Northside Drive to confront him at the shop.

I must have blazed past a cop on the way, because within minutes of my arrival the law was on the scene. Their presence didn't affect me. I was irate and growing angrier by the minute, barking at this dude for stealing from me, an accusation that in reality held little water. Except I wasn't living in reality. I was in a world all my own, one in which everyone in my orbit was plotting against me.

The officers demanded I calm down, but that was background noise. I threw a punch. And then another, and another, beating my friend until a blast of pepper spray hit my eyes. I stumbled backward, the two officers wrestling me to the ground and putting me in handcuffs. I was placed in the back seat of the cruiser but I wasn't done just yet. With my eyes burning, I stomped on the door of the car, so hard that the trim of the vehicle began to break off. An ambulance arrived and I was transported to Grady Hospital Detention Center. After being treated for the pepper spray, I was brought to Fulton County, where I read the list of charges against me.

- Damage to government property
- Obstruction
- Driving without a license
- Reckless driving
- Running a red light or stop sign
- Failure to maintain a lane
- Driving on the wrong side of the road

Damn. I did all that?

I'd get out of lockup the next day, though. Prosecutors dropped every one of those charges citing "for want of prosecution," meaning I was fucked regardless of the incident at the car shop. I was scheduled to go in front of the judge the next month and he now had a laundry list to choose from as to why I belonged in jail. I'd failed another drug test. I'd skipped out on the rehab. I'd gotten rearrested.

When that court date came, my attorneys filed a special plea of mental incompetency, writing that their client was unable "to go forward and/or intelligently participate in the probation revocation hearing." In the past—like when I checked in to the rehab—my lawyers had pulled certain moves with the idea that they would keep me out of jail, but this time it was just the flat-out truth. A plea of mental incompetency was warranted. I'd lost my damn mind.

Fulton County Superior Court judge John J. Goger wasn't sold on that argument. Goger was familiar with my case. Five years earlier he'd sentenced me on my aggravated assault charge after the incident at Big Cat's studio with the pool stick.

"You have a great future in music, but you seem to get in trouble," he'd told me at the time.

Three years later he sentenced me to a year in jail for failing to comply with the terms of my probation. Goger could see I had a problem with drugs, but for him that wasn't an excuse for me to continually break the law. He wanted to put this "mental competency" to the test. I was committed to Anchor Hospital, an Atlanta psychiatric and chemical dependency facility, where I was to undergo a series of evaluations.

Three days later I was discharged. The staff at Anchor Hospital weren't buying my lawyers' claims that I had a serious psychiatric condition. They thought I was using that as an excuse.

The folks at Anchor Hospital may not have believed I was crazy, but the rest of the world was about to be sure of it. Days after being discharged I strolled into Tenth Street Tattoo, a shop around the corner from Patchwerk.

I'd spent the previous night at Patchwerk. Atlanta had gotten hit with one of its biggest snowstorms in years and I got snowed in there.

When I walked into the shop that day I wasn't sure of what I wanted to get. I did know where I wanted it done, though. I walked up to the counter, introduced myself to the owner, pointed to my right cheek, and asked him what we could put there.

My whole body was covered in tattoos. I'd gotten my first when I was nineteen, around the time I'd first started robbing folks and breaking into houses. It was an eyeball on the back of my neck, a reminder to always watch my back. Since then I'd periodically added more.

I already had a bunch of smaller ones on my face but with my skin being so dark, the tattoos under my eyes were hard to make out. I thought it looked like I had two black eyes. I wanted something big, something bold, something unmistakable.

With all I'd been through of late I'd never felt more alienated. I was an outcast, a rebel, a weirdo. More than anything I was tired. Tired of running away from my reputation, tired of trying to convince people I wasn't a bad person. I wanted to embrace being the villain. I wanted to broadcast that I didn't give a fuck what anyone said or thought about me. I'd just gotten a gold grill put in my mouth and I wanted to alter my appearance even more.

"Well, that's cool, man," the shop owner told me. His name was Shane. "But, uh, yeah, I can't really tell you what to put there. Honestly I just have no idea where to start."

I unzipped the orange hoodie I had on to show him my ice cream cone chain.

"What about this?" I asked him. "This is my thing."

Shane drew up my soon-to-be-infamous ice cream cone tattoo. It was perfect. Almost perfect. It needed something else.

"Just make that shit real rock-and-roll," I told him.

With that he added the lightning bolts and the letters "BRRR," and got to work. An hour later, I was out of there and on my way to Patchwerk. I was feeling good about the tattoo. It was what I'd been going for.

That afternoon, the piercer at the shop tweeted out a photo from my visit. The Internet exploded.

"Rapper Gucci Mane has had a large tattoo of a triple-scoop ice cream cone inked onto his face just days after he was released from a mental health facility."

—*Daily Mail*

"Gucci Mane's latest tattoo—an ice cream cone with three scoops and the word 'brrr' across the right side of his face—has appeared all over the internet today. For the most part, people seem shocked and confused by the rapper's unusual decision, and some have questioned whether his recent stay in a mental health facility was a bit too brief."   —*Rolling Stone*

"Whatever they're drinking over at 1017 Brick Squad headquarters, we'll take two and call it a week, thank you."   —*Los Angeles Times*

I knew the tattoo would get a reaction, but I couldn't believe the magnitude of it. When I left the shop I'd been thinking about what the people back at Patchwerk would say when they saw me, not the *New York Daily News*.

People were talking a lot of shit, but the crazy thing is that the response had a positive effect on me. It kind of woke me up. I'd gotten so down on myself that I'd completely lost sight of how many people still cared about what I was up to. I was still a big deal in this industry.

I got back to work, locking in with Drumma Boy for *The Return of Mr. Zone 6*. The title meant something. I knew my stock had fallen and I knew what people were saying about me.

I didn't give a fuck about people saying I'd lost my marbles, but I didn't like that folks were calling *The Appeal* a sellout album, like I'd gone Hollywood working with Pharrell or Swizz or Wyclef. That was wrong. *The Appeal* was a great album with a piss-poor rollout. But how I felt didn't matter much. I needed to remind everyone exactly who I was and where I came from.

Except *The Return of Mr. Zone 6* wasn't a return to my earlier work. The mixtape would mark the beginning of a shift in my sound. I'd always been the one who made trap music fun and colorful, but that Gucci, the one with the memorable ad-libs and different characters, that guy was gone. I couldn't get back to that because it wasn't who I was anymore.

I became so determined to get back into the winner's circle that I lost sight of how making music was supposed to be fun. I was spending more time in the studio than ever before and I was definitely rapping my ass off, but the songs coming out were just different. I was angry. I was resentful. I felt like I'd been dealt a bad hand. I missed Keyshia. As much as I tried to bury those emotions with lean, weed, and reckless spending, they always ended up surfacing, especially in the music.

Damn I think I love her but I don't really know her good
Know I wanna fuck her but really thinkin' if I should
How can I believe her? I don't even believe myself
Tell me how to trust her, I can't even trust myself
But I can't live alone, at the end of the day can't fuck myself
I told her I'm confused and she told me to go fuck myself
Now I'm alone in this world, nothing left for me
But I was born all alone so I guess that's how it's meant to be
But she was sent to me and I didn't recognize
And I blame it on my pride on the fact I'm sittin' in silence
Eyes redder than a rose, heart bluer than a violet
My heart broke and I'm heartless and ain't no need to hide it
                                        —"Better Baby" (2010)

"Something darker," I was telling all my producers. "Give me something darker."

Darker was different, but it was still good music. *The Return of Mr. Zone 6* was a tough album and sold twenty-two thousand copies in its first week with no promotion and a fraction of the budget of *The Appeal*. This was a step in the right direction, but so often in my life, one step forward was followed by two steps back.

•

Two weeks after the release of *The Return of Mr. Zone 6*, I was in Memphis for a show at a club called Level II. Coach came to my hotel and told me I wasn't going to be able to perform. We had to go back to Atlanta, now.

"You've got a warrant out?" he asked. "Something about a girl putting out a battery complaint against you?"

It took a minute, but I realized what Coach was talking about. Back in January I'd pulled up on this chick outside of the South DeKalb Mall. She was leaving the Chick-fil-A and got all excited when she recognized me in my Hummer. She hopped in and we started driving around, talking, but I wasn't much in the mood for talking. I asked her if she wanted to get a hotel room. She declined. Fine by me. It wasn't going to be hard to find another girl to lay up with.

I told her I'd drop her back off at the mall, but this chick started demanding that I take her up to her job in Buckhead. She had some nerve. I wasn't in the mood for that shit that day.

"Look, I'm not a taxi," I told her. "I'll either take you back to the mall or I can drop you off at the bus stop up here."

This girl started cussing and screaming at me to drive her to her job. I'd had enough. I reached across the passenger seat and opened the door.

"You need to get out of my car."

The arguing continued until I put that bitch out of my car, but let me be clear on this. I don't think I put this girl in no danger. But she went out and got herself a lawyer and demanded fifteen thousand dollars, claiming that my car was in motion and she was tumbling down the street or something.

My lawyer said I should just pony up the money and be done with it, but I was already feeling like she played me. Fifteen thousand was petty cash but I didn't want to give her a dime on principle. I should have swallowed my pride, though. Between lawyer fees, a sixty-thousand-dollar settlement that came later down the line, and my time, the incident would cost me a whole lot more than that.

I'd forgotten about the whole thing until Coach told me I couldn't perform in Memphis. After three months, she'd filed a complaint.

I posted the five-thousand-dollar bail but was held for violating my probation in Fulton County. Then, for some reason, I was sent to the Georgia Diagnostic and Classification Prison in Jackson, a facility fifty miles south of Atlanta. I'd only spend three weeks there but these were three of the worst weeks I ever spent locked up.

Jackson State is a diagnostic prison, a waiting room. It's a place where teams of prison officials, counselors, and medical professionals determine which of Georgia's thirty-one state prisons an inmate gets sent to. Unless you're on death row. Then Jackson State's your last stop.

As soon as I got there I had my head shaved. Then I was made to strip naked alongside the rest of the incoming inmates in the intake room, with the COs watching us. After I bent over for a cavity search they sent me to the showers. I was given a small bottle of shampoo and told to apply it not only to my now bald head but to my pubic hair as well. It was lice-killing shampoo.

After the shower I was given a white prison jumpsuit, photographed for my prison ID, and brought to "H House," solitary confinement, where I spent the remainder of my time at Jackson State.

Being in the hole again was horrible. It was sweltering in there. No air circulation at all. And the rats . . . I hadn't been in my cell five minutes when I saw one scurry by with a tail that was longer than me. I swear the rats were the size of cats in that place. I never thought I'd be so happy to be back at Fulton County when I was transferred back three weeks later.

I'd spend another month in county jail before I was freed. Again, I felt like I'd missed a lot. Even though I was only gone for three months—my shortest stretch since my sixty days in DeKalb County a decade earlier—a lot had happened. On the music front, there were two new guys in the city making a lot of noise: 2 Chainz and Future.

I'd known 2 Chainz for fifteen years. He's actually BP's cousin. I knew 2 Chainz from when he was Tity Boi and he was rolling with Ludacris in the nineties. He'd had a taste of fame in 2007 with a song called "Duffle Bag Boy," but he and Dolla Boy, the other nigga in the group Playaz Circle, weren't able to follow it up. But Tity Boi was on his own now and he was going by 2 Chainz. And shit finally seemed to be working out well for him.

Future, on the other hand, was someone I'd met only recently. He was from East Atlanta by Kirkwood, an area they call Lil' Mexico. It's nearby, but in Atlanta you can be two streets over and you're in a totally different neighborhood. He was a few years younger too, so we'd never crossed paths coming up.

Future was the cousin of Rico Wade, from the legendary production team Organized Noize. He'd come up in Atlanta's fabled Dungeon Family, around OutKast and Goodie Mob and Bubba Sparxxx. Back then he was rapping under the name Meathead but now he was Future, and he was rolling with my partner Rocko.

Rocko had introduced us earlier that year at Patchwerk. He had just signed Future to his label A1 Recordings and was adamant about this guy's talent. He told me I needed to fuck with Future's new mixtape *Dirty Sprite*, which he'd just put out. I never got around to doing that. I met Future in the aftermath of everything that happened at the end of 2010 and beginning of 2011, so I had a lot of other stuff going on.

Future had picked up a lot of steam by the time I came home in July. The DJs at Magic City and other Atlanta strip clubs were pumping his music heavy. Drake had just gotten on the remix of his song "Tony Montana." Another song Future was featured on, "Racks," was killing the radio and that was a song Future had written. Rocko was right about the dude.

Behind 2 Chainz and Future's big songs was an up-and-coming beatmaker by the name of Mike WiLL Made It. I knew Mike Will very well. I met him in 2006 when he was a sixteen-year-old Marietta High School junior, trying to shop his beats outside of Patchwerk.

Years ago I'd paid him a stack for a batch of 'em and for a while after that Mike Will was hanging around regularly, cutting his teeth at the studio, honing his craft. You can see a young Mike Will in that 2007 Hood Affairs documentary I did when we were working on "No Pad No Pencil."

At some point Mike Will had a falling-out with Deb. I think she tried to sign him to Mizay and for some reason it didn't work out. But after that Deb had made it a point to keep us from working together, and truthfully she filled my head with all sorts of junk about him too. So I'd kind of been on the "Fuck Mike Will" tip myself. That's why there's a four-year gap when we didn't work together.

Mike Will did well for himself, though. Not only was he playing a major role in the rise of 2 Chainz and Future in Atlanta, but he'd also done a song for Rick Ross and Meek Mill called "Tupac Back" that was big too.

His new moniker, Mike Will Made It, was a throwback to our first days of working together. I'd rapped it on a track called "Star Status":

I be freestylin', not using no pencil
Gucci Mane LaFlare I'm flowin' on this instrumental
Mike Will made it, Gucci Mane slayed it
Star status nigga, everybody upgraded

Coach arranged for Mike Will and I to get back into the studio together. But there was still lingering tension. Making matters worse was that niggas in the studio who knew about our past were cracking jokes and making comments. It kept the vibe fucked-up.

It wasn't until one day when it was just me and Mike Will at Patchwerk that we got back to solid. After that we were in sync. Mike Will had really stepped his game up since '07 and he was giving me some of his hardest beats.

His ringtone was "Ain't No Way Around It," one of the big songs he had with Future.

"You gotta give me some shit like that," I told him.

"Yeah? Well, go in on this," he told me, loading up the next beat.

That song became "Nasty," which Mike Will came up with the hook for. After doing my verse I stepped out of the booth and asked him who else we should get on it.

"Future, bro," he told me. "Future would snap on this."

"You love you some Future, huh?"

The next day Future came through and hopped on "Nasty." A couple of hours later 2 Chainz pulled up and the three of us did another song called "Lost It." Afterward, Future and I were talking and he asked me what I thought about us doing a whole mixtape together.

"Cool," I told him. "Let's do it."

Future couldn't believe it was that easy.

"That's why I fuck with you, Gucci," he said. "Ever since I got in this game shit's never been that simple. But I asked you straight up to do a mixtape and you were down. Simple as that."

"No problem," I told him. "We're already here."

Not only did I fuck with Future's music, but he was certified Zone 6 and that made me even more inclined to work with him. Also I liked what a studio rat this dude was. I recorded every day but I also hit the clubs at night and enjoyed myself. Future didn't leave the studio. All he did was record.

This guy's work ethic was giving me a run for my money, so I knew the two of us would knock out a mixtape in no time. That's exactly what we did. *Free Bricks* was out three weeks to the day I came back from jail.

The tape with Future was a natural move. As was my next release, *Ferrari Boyz,* a joint album with Waka that we'd recorded earlier in the year. It was the collaboration I did after those two that would have people scratching their heads.

I'd been approached by Joie Manda with the idea of doing a joint mixtape with this white chick from Oakland. V-Nasty. I didn't know a thing about the girl, but when Joie told me these folks wanted to pay me a couple of hundred grand, I didn't need to know anything about her. She flew in and we knocked out the mixtape in like three days.

V-Nasty turned out to be a controversial artist, being a white girl who said "nigga," but I thought she was cool and I enjoyed doing that tape. All I did was freestyle over twelve Zay beats. Business as usual. Easy money.

.

In September I pleaded guilty to misdemeanor battery in the incident with the girl in my car. Even though I felt I'd done nothing wrong, my lawyer advised me against trying to fight it. After the year I'd just had I knew he was right. I was the boy who cried wolf by that point. Telling my side of the story would have just pissed off the judge.

I was going to have to do a few months in DeKalb County again. This would be my fourth consecutive fall spent behind bars. Truthfully I was more bothered by the three years' probation they were giving me for this. Almost exactly six years after I was first given six years' probation in Fulton County, they were giving me three more in DeKalb County.

Michael Corleone put it best. Just when I thought I was out, they pulled me back in.

PART THREE

XVIII

I'M UP

I hadn't been home a week when I heard the news that Dunk had been shot and killed.

Dunk was supposed to be with Waka that night but ended up coming to meet me at a recording studio in East Atlanta where we were going to shoot a video for "Push Ups," a song off *BAYTL* he was featured on. I hadn't arrived yet when he got into it with some nigga, who pulled out a strap and shot him. I hated that it happened like that. I hated that Dunk was there that night because of me.

Everybody knew Dunk as Waka's best friend and he was, but he and I were close too. Nobody knows this, but whenever Waka and I were having our problems, Dunk was always the one to get us to patch shit up. He was the bridge between us. The mediator.

I'd left DeKalb County earlier that week, determined to get my career back on track after more than a year of what had been one setback after another. All of that hadn't broken me, though. I was ready to bounce back, but the sudden loss of Dunk could have easily sent me into another downward spiral.

Someone who deserves credit for keeping me on track is Mike Will, whom I'd linked back up with shortly before I went back to jail.

Everybody knows Zay is my go-to producer. The thing is since day one, Zay and I have been each other's biggest fan. I'll rap over whatever beat Zay plays me and whatever I do on there, Zay thinks it's hard as hell. That's just how it's always been with us.

Working with Mike Will is different. Even though he's nearly ten years my junior, Mike Will is highly opinionated with his ideas. He lets you know what he thinks should be happening on any given album, song, verse, or hook. He's a perfectionist. Mike Will will get up from behind the boards and walk into the booth to tell me what he thinks I should be doing differently. I remember Coach told him not to do that when we got back to working together, but Mike Will didn't pay him no mind. The guy has confidence and is an asset in the studio. He pushes me.

The week I came home Mike Will and I locked in at Patchwerk for the making of *Trap Back*. *The Return of Mr. Zone 6* and *Free Bricks* had been steps in the right direction, but I had hiccups having to go back to jail. This one was going to be my comeback mixtape.

I'd written a bunch of raps in jail and started up recording those, but after a few songs Mike Will told me to throw that shit away and get back to freestyling like we'd been doing over the summer. Zay would never say something like that to me.

The other difference between the two is that Mike Will would stay in the studio all night. From day one Zay has always been family first, so if we're not working out of his crib, he's doing a few songs, then going home. Zay doesn't smoke, drink, or shoot dice and he's not about sticking around while I record over other producers' beats. If it was up to him, I'd be recording exclusively over his shit. Mike Will's not like that. He'll be there the whole night, regardless of whether it's his beats I'm rapping on or Zay's or Drumma Boy's or Sonny Digital's or whoever's. And he's always got an opinion on what's going on.

"Man, I don't really like how you did those ad-libs," he'd tell me. "You really need to do those over."

"I know you can make something harder than that. Let's get back to the old Gucci."

There are not a lot of folks comfortable talking to me like that and truthfully I like it that way. Mike Will has me feeling like this shit is a job sometimes. Recording is supposed to be fun, and redoing verses and ad-libs is not my idea of a good time. It's not something I typically do. But when we were working on *Trap Back* I could tell that Mike Will wanted to see me come back and win just as bad as I wanted it. He knew what time it was. When the tape dropped a month later the hard work proved to be worthwhile.

"*Trap Back* is easily the strongest release from Gucci Mane since, possibly, 2008. On this project Gucci sounds clear, concise, and back focused on his career."

—*AllHipHop.com*

"With *Trap Back*, Gucci Mane is back in his element. He's removed himself from the curiosity of *BAYTL* and returned to the vice-indulging-laced lyrics and the system-shattering soundscapes that fueled his initial ascent. Bundle up." —*XXL*

"The other reason *Trap Back* is great is the increasingly prominent Atlanta producer Mike Will Made It, who continues to demonstrate that he has an ear for the smallest details that make a simple rap song a great rap song. His sound is like a Flubberized blending of Zaytoven's 8-bit pings and Drumma Boy's funeral marches: it's menacing and playful all at once, which means it's a perfect match for Gucci's style. In a development that really shouldn't have taken this long, he flips the *Tetris* theme into trap music for Gucci to rap on for 'Get It Back.' The instrumental could serve as a neatly boiled-down synopsis of Gucci's style: simple, deceptively absorbing, maddeningly addictive, frantically paced. Drumma Boy also swings by, and Zaytoven contributes some of his gangsta tinker-toy productions. The result isn't a revelation exactly, but it's the most recognizably Gucci-ish Gucci release in some time."

—*Pitchfork*

It was true. For the first time in a long time, I was starting to feel like me again.

The biggest record on *Trap Back* was "Plain Jane," which Mike Will produced and Rocko was featured on. This shit killed the streets. The love I was getting from the critics was great, but I was seeing the impact of "Plain Jane" in Atlanta and every other

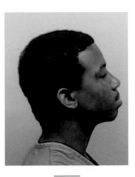

25   26

29

30

31

34

35

city I went to. It was fucking people up. It never got serviced to radio or made an official single, but to this day I can't do a show without performing "Plain Jane." It became an immediate fan favorite.

The response from "Plain Jane" and *Trap Back* on the whole got me going again. I wasn't where I wanted to be but I was on my way. Shit just felt like it was getting back. On top of the music I had gotten an offer to be in a movie.

I had signed on to do *Spring Breakers* a year before. I was in Bloomington, Minnesota, for a show and was walking through the Mall of America when my cell phone rang. It was Mariah Carey.

Mariah and I had gotten cool when we did "Obsessed" in 2009, but she had never called me out of the blue before. I knew that she was pregnant with twins and supposed to be giving birth any day now, so I wondered what could be so important for her to be calling me.

"Gucci, do you remember Brett Ratner?" she asked me. "He's the guy who directed the music video for 'Obsessed'? He wants to put you in this movie. This could be a great opportunity for you."

Brett Ratner wasn't the director of *Spring Breakers,* though. It was a guy named Harmony Korine. Apparently he was a huge fan of mine. He'd asked Brett, a friend of his, to get in touch with me for this role. Harmony's name didn't register with me at first but then I found out this was the guy who made the crazy, fucked-up movie *Kids* in the nineties. I'd seen another film of his too, *Gummo.* Both those movies were some dark, twisted shit but I'd liked 'em.

Harmony wanted me in *Spring Breakers* so badly that he post-poned filming until after my two little stints in jail in 2011, and he was going to pay me a whole bunch of money to play the role of Archie. Archie was the bad guy, the former friend turned foe of the main character Alien, played by James Franco. His name I knew. This was a major motion picture. I didn't need to know much more. Sign me up.

I spent two weeks in St. Petersburg, Florida, filming *Spring Breakers.* Harmony got his money's worth out of me. I had no idea making a movie would be so time-consuming. We were working twelve-hour days and then I was going out at night on top of that for shows and appearances.

The last scene I shot was my big sex scene and by that point I was exhausted. There had been pounds of this fake herbal weed on set, but that junk gave me a headache, so I stuck to smoking Kush and of course I was drinking lean too. It was four in the morning and even with these two naked bad bitches on me—one riding me while the other sucked my toes—I couldn't keep my eyes open. I was knocked out, snoring in the middle of the movie set. Harmony kept having to wake me up for takes. Somehow I managed to wake up long enough to ad-lib what has got to be one of the best lines of that whole movie.

I feel like you're playing Mozart on my dick.

Even though I was high as hell the whole time I did *Spring Breakers,* I got a lot out of that experience. To work with a di-rector as talented as Harmony and play opposite James Franco in my first film was a blessing. I learned a lot watching James Franco do his thing. The whole way he approached his character was superimpressive. He was all in, fully immersed as Alien. He played the hell out of that role. He knew his craft like I knew the rap game.

Working with the girls was great too. Rachel Korine shared her husband's love for my music and Ashley Benson wanted to take a photo with my chain on. Despite crazy rumors that came out that something happened with me and Selena Gomez, we never even met during the making of the movie. We didn't share any scenes together. Regardless, I appreciated her part in it. The whole thing was just a positive working environment. A good vibe. Harmony was a hard boss but it made for a dope movie. And he also turned out to be a cool person. He became a friend for life during our time working together.

Spring Breakers inspired me to get on my Gucci Spielberg shit. Within a month of my return to Atlanta I started production on a hood comedy called *The Spot,* which I starred in and played producer on. I brought Boomtown on to direct it and had Rocko, Keyshia, and a bunch of local Atlanta comedians acting alongside me. I even got the two crazy white boys from *Spring Breakers*—the ATL Twins—to be in it.

After that it was back to music. In May I put out another tape, *I'm Up,* because that's how I was feeling. I was the old cocky Gucci again. *I'm Up* had a bunch of bangers on there with features from Wayne, Rick Ross, and Chris Brown. And this was just for my mixtape. The label wasn't paying for these features and it wasn't costing me a dime either. These people just wanted to work with me. I even had T.I. on that tape and he and I hadn't been cool for years.

I was in Patchwerk's Studio A, putting the finishing touches on the tape. Meanwhile T.I. was in Studio B doing his thing. Between the two studios his bodyguard and one of my partners were shooting the breeze. They were longtime friends. Eventually my buddy brought Tip's bodyguard to Studio A and a short while after that T.I. came in looking for his security.

T.I. and I had not spoken in a long time. We'd had our fair share of issues, but when we started chopping it up it was like the first day we'd met on the set of the "3 Kings" video a decade earlier. Like me, T.I. had gone through a lot in the years since. He had spent time locked up and experienced his own ups and downs. I sensed we were both over any beef.

We agreed to do a song together. Given our history, that would be something that would shock a lot of people. This was like what Jeezy and I had planned on doing but it hadn't worked out. Maybe this time it would.

I played T.I. two songs but he said he wanted something bigger.

"Well, I do got a big record," I told him. "But it's already out."

"Let me hear it," he responded.

I played "Plain Jane" and then T.I. had me run it back and play it again. After the second run-through he was ready to go. He hit the booth and recorded a verse on the spot. I had already filmed a music video for the song with Rocko, Waka, and Mike Will, but it wasn't out yet. T.I. said he'd be down to shoot a scene for his verse separately that we could put in there. The whole thing came together quick.

At the end of the summer I flew out to LA with Coach for a business trip. It was a crazy week. Harmony and I met up to do some last-minute voice-over work for *Spring Breakers* and he let me check out a raw cut of the movie. The shit came out amazing.

The next day I had an all-day photo shoot for the streetwear brand LRG, and this was not a typical photo shoot. The company rented out this mansion where they had me doing all sorts of wild stuff—fishing out of the bathtub, eating from a huge pile of burgers, shooting dice on the marble staircase. This collection was called "High-End Lowlifes." The concept was to have me doing all this hood-ass shit in a crib that defined opulence.

I decided I was going to double dip on this mansion. I'd made this song "Fuck Da World" with Future and I had a good feeling about it. I was hot again, Future was coming up, and Mike Will had the Midas touch. Every beat he made was blowing up. All the pieces were there. Future happened to be in LA that week so I hit him and told him I had this crazy spot for us to shoot a video for "Fuck Da World." The thing was we had to do it right now. Future put whatever he was doing on hold and came through.

Of course I didn't have permission to film a music video in this house and I had no intention of putting up the money or going through the proper channels to do so. I was just going to piggyback off this LRG shoot.

When the whole mob showed up—Future, his people, the video production crew, the models—the homeowner and the LRG crew went crazy. But it was too late. I'd made up my mind we were getting footage at this spot.

"Keep the camera rolling," I told the videographer. "Don't listen to what these folks say."

The most important part of that trip to California was my meeting with Todd. I wanted to show him I'd gotten my shit together and that I deserved a chance to make things right with the label. Todd and I had never had any sort of beef or fallout, but he and I had become distant after how everything played out with *The Appeal*. I'd been so embarrassed that I didn't want to go to Todd until I had something to show. With *Trap Back, I'm Up, Spring Breakers,* and this next mixtape I had on the way, now was the time.

"I'm sorry, Todd," I told him. "I'm sorry for the last year and I'm sorry for the last album. I've cleaned myself up."

We hugged it out. That deep friendship was still there. Our relationship was bigger than business. Still, there was business I wanted to attend to. I wanted to restructure my deal at Warner Bros. We needed to get a proper budget for my next album like I'd gotten with *The Appeal*.

Todd told me his hands were tied as far as restructuring my contract, but he gave me the green light to sell my mixtapes on iTunes to put some extra money in my pocket. He also had another idea.

"You should start calling yourself the trap god," he said. "Actually . . . you should legally change your name to Trap God."

Legally change my name? Todd was crazy, but he was onto something.

"Okay, it's perfect!" he said. "Put together a mixtape called *Trap God* and I'll sign off on it so you can sell it on iTunes."

That's how the Trap God moniker was born.

Coming up with the Trap God name and letting me sell my mixtapes would be the last things Todd did for me at Warner Bros. A month after I put out the project he resigned from his position as CEO of the label. Not long after, Warner Bros. folded its urban music department and by default I was transferred to Atlantic Records.

These were the folks who screwed me in 2007 with *Back to the Trap House* and now I was supposed to deal with them again.

I hadn't gotten what I wanted out of my conversation with Todd, one of my biggest supporters, so I knew it wasn't going to go any better at Atlantic. And I was right about that. We couldn't see eye to eye on anything.

Fuck it.

Everything had been going so well. I wasn't going to let the label mess it up. I didn't need 'em. I'd get my contract sorted out later. For now I was on strike with Atlantic Records and taking my career back into my own hands.

XIX

BRICK BY BRICK

Patchwerk had always been my spot, but my bills there had gotten ridiculous. Studio fees were running me nearly a hundred thousand dollars a year. If I wasn't on the road, I was there. Every day. After I signed Waka, I'd started renting out both rooms of the studio at $150 an hour each. Even when I wasn't recording I'd be there just hanging. But the meter was always running. I don't even want to think about how many hours I got billed just to be smoking weed and drinking lean at Patchwerk.

So when I decided I was on strike with the label and they were no longer footing the bill, I decided to set up my own shop. I scouted a couple of locations and landed on a studio in the heart of East Atlanta. I named it the Brick Factory, after the Hit Factory in Miami, which had always been one of my favorite places to record.

The Brick Factory was the studio where Dunk had gotten

killed. Because of that I had reservations about getting the place. Financially, though, it made sense.

I needed to get rid of the bad vibes in there and give it a fresh start. With the help of Beasley, a longtime friend who doubled as my hood secretary of sorts, I had the whole spot gutted and remodeled. I put a lot of money into it. There was a lounge with flat-screen TVs. A workout room. I had my own little apartment-like area with a bedroom and kitchen and shower upstairs. And I assigned Zay the task of outfitting the three recording rooms with top-of-the-line equipment. We made it real nice. I also bought the car wash next door and had the fence between the buildings torn down. My plan was to add two more recording rooms after we finished phase one of renovations.

I already had a reputation as an A&R man—someone with an ear for new talent. My early involvement with Waka, OJ, Nicki, and Mike Will spoke for itself. But the Brick Factory was where I took an active role in grooming the careers of the next genera-tion of young talent coming out of Atlanta.

.

Having this multiroom recording studio allowed for that. Before, anyone who was in one of my sessions at Patchwerk was there to be a part of whatever I was working on. Now, with three rooms and two more on the way, there was space for everyone to work on their own stuff simultaneously. I could bounce around and get involved in what everyone had going on. I wanted my studio to be a place where artists had the freedom to experiment. A place to take chances. Where people could be themselves but also find themselves as rappers or producers. For me this was a much deeper level of involvement. I'd set up an incubator of talent.

I'd had this in mind when I got the place. I wanted a new stable of protégés. Waka and I were on okay terms, but he had his own career now so he wasn't around all the time. That meant Wooh and Frenchie weren't around either. And Dunk was dead. So I was looking for a new crew of young bulls to take under my wing.

Even before I got the studio, I'd been on the hunt for artists who would be good fits for 1017. First was Scooter. Young Scooter and I had gotten cool during the summer of 2011 when I was working with Future on *Free Bricks*. Future and Scooter were childhood friends from Kirkwood. I mentioned earlier that I never knew Future coming up, but when he introduced Scooter and me at Patchwerk, it turned out he and I had actually met before.

"Don't you remember me, bro?" he asked. "From that dice game in East Atlanta?"

Come to think of it, I did remember this guy. We'd met maybe a year or two back one day when I was hangin' in my old neighborhood. He'd been with some of my old partners from the Zone 6 Clique. At the time I didn't know he rapped, but I did figure he must have some street in him to be there gamblin' with my old partners. They didn't hang with anyone who didn't.

When Future reintroduced us I immediately took a liking to Scooter. He was pretty green when it came to the music. I don't think Scooter had even put out a mixtape yet. But I liked his approach. There was an effortlessness to it. Lackadaisical. Almost like he wasn't even rapping. Like Scooter was just talking on tracks.

I'd wanted to get Future to sign with Brick Squad, but by that point I'd come to terms with the fact that that wasn't going to happen. Future already had his situation with Rocko, and he was so hot that summer that his major-label deal was coming any day. I'd missed the boat on Future, but it was still early for Scooter.

"I'm telling you he hard, Gucci," Future told me. "You should sign him."

Scooter and I kept in touch and a year later, after he got himself a buzz in the city off a song called "Colombia," we put it on paper and made it official. Scooter was now a 1017 Brick Squad artist.

Then there was Young Dolph.

I linked with Dolph through Drumma Boy, who put me in touch with him for a feature at some point in 2011. But I was sleeping on Dolph then. I did a lot of features for lesser-known rappers in the South. A lot of the time these were dudes who already had money in the streets—which was how they could afford a feature from me—and were now looking to give it a go in the rap game. So I did a verse for Dolph and that was that.

Months later I was hanging out with one of my partners from Mobile, Alabama, when he asked me if I fucked with the nigga Dolph from South Memphis whom I'd done that song with. At first I didn't even know who he was talking about.

"Well, Dolph got a serious following out here in Alabama," he told me. "You really should fuck with him."

He had Dolph's new mixtape—*A Time 2 Kill*—in his car. I gave it a listen on the drive to Atlanta and I was impressed. With him it was his voice. Superdistinct. Superdeep. I knew how far a voice could take you in the game, so I hit Drumma for Dolph's number and told him the next time he made it to Atlanta he should pull up on me at Patchwerk.

My buddy was right about Dolph's movement too. This was not some unknown up-and-comer with nothing to show. He already had money and his own independent thing going. That would keep us from doing a deal with 1017, but Dolph and I ended up getting tight anyway. He was just a real nigga. When I got the new studio I made sure he knew he was welcome to pull up and work anytime he wanted.

I was checking in on the renovations at the Brick Factory one day when one of my partners started telling me about Peewee Longway.

"Gucci you know the dude Peewee from Zone Three?" he said. "The nigga who rap?"

"*Peewee*?" I thought. "From Jonesboro South?"

"That nigga."

"Yeah I know Peewee," I said. "He don't rap, though."

"Well, he rap now."

I had not seen Peewee in many years, but I'd known him for quite some time. Peewee repped Zone 3, on the Westside of Atlanta. We always ran in different circles coming up, but I would see him frequently at the Libra. I'm talking way, way, way back when I was twenty-three, performing at their open mic nights. But Peewee was never rapping at the Libra. He was always there just as a patron of the club. From what I knew of him, Peewee was strictly a hustler.

As soon as I heard that Peewee was a rapper—the "Longway" part was new—I sent for him to come to my studio. I was signing him to Brick Squad. That might sound odd, but it's a good example of something else that I look for in artists.

Peewee was always this little, funny, charming nigga whom people just seemed to gravitate toward. Everyone I knew liked

Peewee and he was very much respected from his dealings in the streets. So I didn't really need to hear Peewee's music to know I wanted to sign him. The music was the easy part. That shit I could help him out with. And once I did, I already knew Peewee was someone who would be well received in Atlanta.

I had twenty-five thousand dollars in cash waiting for him when he came to the studio a few days later. But Peewee had other plans.

"You ain't even got to worry about paying me, bro," he said. "What I really want is for you to sign my young boys here."

"I'm pretty much set on signing you, Peewee," I told him. "But if this is what you really want, then tell me about your boys."

That's when Peewee introduced me to Young Thug. Not only had I never met Thug, but I'd never heard a word about him. But I took a look at this tall, skinny kid with a bunch of tattoos on his face like me and I got the feeling he could be something. He definitely had a look.

Peewee wanted me to sign Thug as part of a three-man crew, but it was clear who the diamond in the rough was. So I took the twenty-five thousand I'd had ready for Peewee, gave it to Young Thug, and signed him on the spot. I hadn't known him longer than thirty minutes.

I'd taken a chance on Thug but it didn't take long for me to realize he was something special. Thug started coming to the studio every day, staying for days on end, and man, listen . . . the boy was going fucking crazy. I remember Thug had some shit going with his teeth and was wearing some type of mask over his mouth for a brief period. When he would take it off to record it would be like Scorpion from *Mortal Kombat* pulling his mask off and breathing fire. He was bouncing off the walls. He had different voices, different flows, and he was switching in and out of 'em effortlessly. I remember when he made "2 Cups Stuffed." It was obvious Thug was a superstar in the making. All he needed from me was a little seasoning.

·

A few weeks later I was at Zay's crib when he waved me out of the booth to show me something on the computer.

"Check this out." He laughed. "There's some boys here who sound just like you and they're rapping over some beats that sound just like mine."

Zay was watching a music video for a song called "Bando" by a three-man group calling themselves Migos. He was right. There were similarities. Like Zay and I had first started doing a decade earlier these boys were talking about cookin' up work in the kitchen and they were making it fun. It was upbeat. Animated. Catchy. Silly. Right away I liked what Migos were doing.

Later in the day I was back at the Brick Factory showing the "Bando" video to Scooter, Thug, and Peewee. I found a booking number in the description on YouTube and called it. Whoever answered couldn't believe it was me.

"Get the fuck out of here, man," I was told. "This ain't no Gucci Mane."

"Well, if this ain't Gucci, then tell those boys not to come down to 1074 Memorial Drive because Gucci Mane don't want to sign 'em."

They were on their way.

Migos were from Gwinnett County, north of Atlanta, so it

took them an hour or so to get to the studio. When they did show up, it was just two of them. The third, Offset, was locked up in DeKalb County on a parole violation.

The first thing I noticed about these boys was that they had on a bunch of fake-ass jewelry. I took two gold necklaces off my neck, gave one to each of them, and told them I wanted them to be on my label. I'd taken out forty-five thousand dollars, fifteen thousand for each of them. Quavo and Takeoff were on board, but I needed to make sure the third guy, Offset, was too. I wanted this group as I'd first seen them, as a trio.

They got Offset on the phone from jail. He didn't need much convincing. I asked him what he wanted me to do with his share of the money and he told me to hold on to it for him until he got out. And with that Migos were on Brick Squad. Quavo and Takeoff headed home with plans to return the next day and get to work.

Shortly after Migos left, Scooter called me out of the booth while I was recording. There was something I needed to see.

"You see those boys threw their jewelry in the trash can?"

I figured Scooter was trying to be funny, making a joke about those bullshit chains. But I looked in the trash can and sure enough, there they were. Quavo and Takeoff had thrown out their old chains after I'd given them real jewelry. We had a laugh at that one.

Migos would be the last addition to the new team. I came so close to signing Yung Fresh—who later started going by Bankroll Fresh—too, but his parents got involved in the negotiations and the deal fell apart. That one bummed me out 'cause I'd been cool with Fresh since '07 and thought he was a hell of a talent. We ended up tearing up the contract and Fresh gave the advance back save for a couple of Gs I told him to keep to take care of some probation shit he had going on. I guess there's always going to be the ones who got away.

The Brick Factory was now up and running with a team of hungry, talented prospects following my lead. The studio took on a life of its own. At any given time, someone would be in there working. At full capacity there might be thirty people in the building. I might be in one room with C4 or Honorable C.N.O.T.E. working on *Trap House 3* while Thug was in the next, recording his *1017 Thug* mixtape with one of the 808 Mafia producers. Or Metro Boomin might be in a room just cookin' up some beats by himself. Or Migos might be downstairs doing their own thing. Scooter and Waka were both on the road a lot then, but whenever they were in town they'd be there too. Even the artists who never officially signed with me were always welcome and I did mixtapes with all of them—*East Atlanta Memphis* with Dolph, *Money Pounds Ammunition* with Peewee, *Trust God Fuck 12* with Rich Homie Quan.

It was a 24/7 operation with an open-door policy for any rapper or producer I fucked with to come be a part of what we had going on. I gave those boys hell whenever they tried to leave. Take a nap on the couch if you tired, I'd tell 'em. If one of the engineers got tired, I'd sit down and record Peewee or Thug myself. If you need a break from recording, let's roll something up. Or pour something up. Or shoot some dice. Ain't no need to leave the studio.

The Brick Factory was some hippie commune shit. Outlaws playing by our own set of rules. A tale of true American counterculture.

•

After spending the winter getting the studio set up and my signees off the ground, I started spring with a trip to California for the *Spring Breakers* premiere. Keyshia was joining me. I'd been asking her to take me back for months and she finally agreed to come on the trip and see if our relationship was worth another shot.

She'd seen I'd gotten my act together and was proud of me. I'd promised her I was done drinking lean, which was a lie, but as long as I stayed on point and didn't let things spiral out of control she would have no reason not to believe me. To be safe, I'd started mixing my lean with fruit punch or some other colored drink so she wouldn't see a photo or video out there of me sipping. Keyshia was an angel. She didn't know the first thing about lean. As long as I wasn't drinking something purple, she wouldn't have cause for concern.

The premiere went great. Not only did people seem to like the film but I was getting a lot of love for my part in particular. I was glad Keyshia was there to see that. It brought us back to how things were when we first fell for each other. Me on point and feeling good about myself, not falling apart from the drugs and out of my mind.

Harmony had us seated in the theater next to Marilyn Manson and his girlfriend at the time, Lindsay. Harmony and Marilyn were buddies, and Harmony thought the two of us would hit it off. Harmony swung by our seats to introduce us, but as it turned out Marilyn and I had already met on the red carpet earlier.

Lindsay complimented Keyshia on her lipstick and the two of them struck up a conversation.

"Looks like we both got us some fancy bitches," was the first thing Marilyn Manson said to me.

The four of us hit it off and ended up hanging the rest of the night. Marilyn and I chopped it up about music and our shared love for the city of Miami. After the movie we hit an after-party, and after the after-party, Marilyn and I hit a studio where we made "Fancy Bitch," a song inspired by our first interaction. Marilyn Manson turned out to be a cool, down-to-earth dude. I didn't know a lot about him beyond his wild persona in music. I respected how he could let his guard down and be a regular person when the camera wasn't rolling. In the rap game there are so many people who feel like they need to keep the tough-guy shit going 24/7 and can't even hold a conversation.

Things were going good in LA, but back home a storm was brewing. While I was away Waka had showed up at the studio, trying to get the files for a song he and I had made. One of the engineers working there told Waka he didn't have permission to give up songs off the hard drive. He told Waka to wait until I got back into town to sort it out. Waka couldn't accept that and he punked him out in front of everyone at the studio and took the files.

I didn't hear about the incident until I got back, and when I did I called Waka and told him not to come to the Brick Factory anymore. He and I initially exchanged words through text but eventually we both made our feelings public.

Waka Flacka flames officially dropped off brick squad 1017. Big Guwop say give me a offer fa this disloyal lil nigga

—@Gucci1017

Somebody tell Gucci Mane 2 SUCK A DICK.
                                    —*@WakaFlockaBSM*

A disagreement over this song was not the end of the world, but it wasn't about the song. It was longtime tension reaching its breaking point. Waka and I had been having problems on and off for three years. But we'd been able to keep it between us, whether that meant fighting it out in the house in Henry County or going months without speaking. Our problems now being broadcast turned everything up a notch and made it harder to patch things up.

Somebody from the label tried to defuse the situation by claiming my Twitter account had been hacked, but nobody was buying it. When asked about it in interviews I did my best to not fuel the fire, admitting we'd had an argument but that we'd work it out in the end. But Waka wasn't doing the same, telling MTV I was jealous of him and that we'd never work together again.

On March 27, a week and a half after Waka and I fell out, I turned myself in to the Fulton County Sheriff's Office on charges of aggravated assault. A US soldier was claiming I'd struck him across the head with a champagne bottle at Harlem Nights. But that incident didn't happen on March 27. It happened at 1:00 a.m. the night of March 16, a few hours after I told the world I was dropping Waka.

"We're just asking that a bond be set," my lawyer said to the judge. "I never ask for an amount. That's not my job. My job is to ask for bond. The conditions I leave to the court's discretion."

"Well, in the exercise of *my* discretion . . ." the judge began.

That was not a good start.

"I understand your position, Mr. Findling, but this gentleman does have an aggravated battery with a deadly weapon just a few years ago and he's already on probation for a battery charge. Now he's been charged with aggravated battery and aggravated assault."

No bond. I sat in Fulton County Jail for another two weeks until my next court date. When that day came I was given a seventy-five-thousand-dollar bond, which I paid only to immediately be arrested and transferred to DeKalb County Jail for violating my probation.

Here we go again.

•

Nobody thought I was getting out after that. Again the consensus was that it was finally a wrap for Gucci. So it didn't surprise me when I heard the artists I'd spent the last six months grooming were trying to defect on me.

Migos had gotten hot quick. Drake had hopped on their song "Versace" and it was out of there. My partner Pee told me they were looking to do a deal with Fly Kix, a guy who had just signed a bunch of new rappers in the city like Rich Homie Quan and Trinidad Jame$.

Scooter, despite being locked up in DeKalb County on his own probation violation, had the attention of the majors in NYC. "Colombia" had made it out of Atlanta. Unfortunately for Scooter, he'd not only signed paperwork with me but at some point he'd signed something with Future's label Freebandz. So his situation was complicated. It was still early for Thug, but things were looking good for him ever since he dropped the

1017 Thug tape. I had so much belief in him that I knew it was only a matter of time before he and I had some contract issues to work out.

And then there was everything with Waka. He wanted off 1017 and I was ready to let him go too. Maybe one day we could be friends again but businesswise it was time for us both to move on. But it wasn't that easy. Unlike with Thug, Scooter, and Migos, Waka's contract with me involved Atlantic Records, and I'd had zero contact with them since I got transferred back there from Warner Bros. at the end of 2012. I knew even if I did sit down with them to figure out Waka's situation, that meeting wasn't going to go the way I wanted it to.

"Gucci, we'd never do that," Quavo told me when I called him from jail to tell him what I'd heard about Migos and Fly Kix. "We loyal to you."

I knew that wasn't true. But I understood it wasn't the best time to be an artist on 1017. The CEO was locked up with no re-lease date in sight. I got that and I didn't take it personally. Most of these boys were dead broke when I met them, so it wasn't hard to believe they'd try to jump ship at a chance to put some more money in their pocket. Still, I'd invested a lot in these artists, so them trying to up and leave was fucking up my business. That part would definitely have to get sorted out.

When I beat the odds and got released from DeKalb County Jail three weeks after my arrest, I didn't call up any of them. I'd deal with the insubordination later. I had *Trap House 3* on the way and I'd made the decision to bump up its release date so I could put it out ahead of Memorial Day weekend.

To me, *Trap House 3* was the culmination of my comeback, a return to form that started when I came home from jail in 2011 and locked in with Mike Will for *Trap Back*. *Trap House 3* was some of the hardest music I'd made in years and I just knew that if I could get people listening to it as they headed down to Miami or Puerto Rico or Myrtle Beach for Black Bike Week, this album would be the soundtrack of their summer. The sooner everyone heard *Trap House 3*, the sooner they were going to get talking about my music again and not the incident at Harlem Nights or my problems with Waka.

I was released under the stipulation that I wear an ankle monitor and remain under house arrest when I wasn't traveling for work. When I accepted those terms, I listed the studio as my residence instead of my apartment in Atlantic Station so that I could still record. I wouldn't have been able to go to the Brick Factory otherwise, so at first this seemed like a good move. But trapping myself at the studio proved to be a terrible decision.

•

Over time the Brick Factory vibe had changed. It had become a hangout more than a place of creation and business. Me and the artists I was working with were a fraction of the bodies there. Everyone's crew had made it a home base too. The fact that the Brick Factory was in the middle of my old neighborhood made things more problematic. I was now seeing a lot of my old partners from the Zone 6 Clique. Every one of them was still heavy in the streets, so it was only a matter of time before everyone's beefs started spilling into my studio. Other people's altercations and issues inadvertently became mine. And I couldn't leave.

Kori Anders, my longtime engineer at Patchwerk, had that luxury, and as tensions escalated at the Brick Factory he started coming by less. Kori was a professional and had no interest in being around that type of stuff. He decided not to be. That's how Sean Paine, an intern from Patchwerk, became the head engineer at my studio.

Back at Patchwerk, Sean had been the engineer who let me and my crew smoke in the studio. He'd roll blunts while I was in the booth and run to the store and grab Swishers or sodas for us to pour up into. I knew he would be a good fit at the Brick Factory.

Sean didn't mind being around some scary shit. And a bunch of scary shit was about to happen.

XX

A NIGHTMARE ON MORELAND

The response to *Trap House 3* was positive. I knew it would be. The album wasn't doing anything crazy numbers-wise, but because I'd put it out independently I was seeing more money on every copy sold. Really what mattered was that people were fucking with the music. My grand experiment with the Brick Factory was paying off.

But I couldn't enjoy *Trap House 3*'s success. I was growing increasingly more anxious. I had an open assault case. A probation violation hearing on the horizon. Defecting artists. My old rap beefs were back on. The unease at the studio made me stress. And as it always did, my stress manifested itself as intense dread and paranoia.

Much of this paranoia was the product of the drugs—delusions brought on by weed and promethazine and codeine syrup coursing through me. I was always high. But there was a legitimacy to my fears as well. My mind was unraveling, no doubt about it, but I really was in the same studio my friend got killed in. I'd experienced people with guns looking to kill me before. I was legally confined to this building, which was in a neighborhood where I'd accumulated a lot of enemies over the past twenty years. That shit was real.

I couldn't sleep. So I drank more lean and smoked more weed. My intake was beyond anything before and my addiction had become unsustainably expensive. The lean was a thousand dollars a pint and I was drinking almost a pint a day. The weed was a few hundred dollars an ounce and I was smoking an ounce a day. More than a grand a day on drugs alone. And those were just the basic necessities. Anything else I came across—Percocets, Xanax bars, molly, whatever really—would get tossed in the mix too.

The money I was sinking into drugs was the least of my concerns. I *needed* this stuff. It was the only thing that could calm me, even if it was temporary. When I did catch some sleep, it wasn't like I was tucked in bed for a restful night. I was nodding out during recording sessions. I was falling out of chairs. I would take too much of something and throw it up. Things were getting bad again. I could feel it. But I didn't know how to stop it.

The studio got broken into. I found out who it was when I reviewed the surveillance footage. When I told them I didn't want them coming by anymore, it didn't go well. Now I had problems with niggas who stayed right around the corner. Niggas with very little to lose.

Earlier in the summer I'd done an interview where I called

my new studio the Fort Knox of the hood. At the time I'd said it in jest because of the gate and surveillance cameras. But now the Brick Factory looked more like an armory than a place where music was made. There were guns everywhere. I could see the look on people's faces when they came through. My studio was no longer a fun place to be. Onetime regulars were dropping like flies.

•

I was still recording like hell. I'd dropped three mixtapes at once—the *World War 3: Molly, Gas,* and *Lean* series—and now I was working on a new project. *Diary of a Trap God.* A lot of the songs on there—"Decapitated," "Half," "High Power Cowards," "Keep It Real"—were recorded during my darkest days, trapped in my brick prison. I was slurring my words bad on those songs. I'd never sounded so congested.

It was the sound of somebody at the end of the line, facing a decision: accept defeat or go down in a blaze. I was sure someone was going to kill me or that I was going to have to kill someone again. That wasn't a difficult decision for me to make.

> *I fell out with my right-hand man, he tried to top on me*
> *I guess it's clear we ain't homies like I think we homies*
> *I'm at the top and I swear to God, it's really lonely*
> *But I'm not coming down, no stoopin' down, I keep it movin'*
> *These young niggas got no respect who make music*
> *Broke-ass nigga, never can get used to it*
> *And the bottom of Sun Valley don't do it like the top do it*
> *Bouldercrest we hear AK's more than church music*
> —"Decapitated" (2013)

Zay was at the studio the night I made "Decapitated." It was late and there wasn't a light on in there save for the glow of Pro Tools coming from the computer monitor. When the beat wasn't playing you could hear a pin drop in there. Dark and quiet. Everyone was gone. Just me and Zay. Like old times. Simpler times.

That was an eerie night. The calm before the storm.

•

Diary of a Trap God was so fucking deep. It needed to be an album, not just another mixtape. To do that I was going to have to reconnect with the people at my label. I needed them to sign off on it being a retail release and I wanted to restructure my deal. I also wanted them to buy out Waka's contract.

My lawyer got in touch with Craig Kallman and Julie Greenwald, the CEO and COO at Atlantic, and came back with an offer. It wasn't to my liking. I marked the contract up with changes and sent it back.

"We can't make any revisions," I was told. "Take it or leave it."

The next day I hopped on Twitter and told Craig and Julie to suck my dick and that was the end of negotiations. The label had its limits too.

Gucci Mane Is No Longer on Atlantic Records

—Fader

•

Telling off Craig and Julie was one of the many ways I was airing grievances on Twitter that week. I was letting it fly. Any shit I felt had been bubbling beneath the surface, whether it was recent or an unresolved situation that had been dormant for years, I put it out there. Now we ain't gotta dance around shit no more, was my thinking. Anyone and everyone could get it. And they did.

Eventually my other lawyer called and told me to stop. I had several pending cases and I was out here threatening folks for anyone to see.

"What are you thinking?!" he told me. "Stop it immediately."

I did stop. And put out word that my Twitter account had been hacked. But then I started to question my lawyer's motives. Did he tell me that 'cause he was looking out for me, or was he doing someone else's bidding? Over the next forty-eight hours my fears festered as I sat in the studio, smoking and drinking lean.

Fuck it.

I'd just fired my entertainment attorney after the failed talks with Atlantic. My criminal lawyer could go too. And I was going to his office to get paperwork to show he no longer represented me. I didn't know what the fuck he was out here doing on my behalf.

I got into it with the security officers at the office and the police were called. My lawyer asked me to leave and when the cops went inside to gather my belongings for me, they found a loaded handgun in the area. I told them it wasn't mine.

My lawyer didn't say anything different.

I think they call that attorney-client privilege. Maybe I was wrong about this guy. Good thing he didn't sign those termination papers.

·

My days were numbered. The cops had let me go but they'd taken the pistol to be fingerprinted and turned into evidence. And I'd already violated the terms of my house arrest simply by leaving my residence and going there.

The next twenty-four hours was a blur. I knew my time was ticking and you could say I made the most of it. I was the East Atlanta bogeyman, making my way through the hood one volatile incident after another. From the Texaco to the barbershop, the whole neighborhood was buzzing about my one-man wrecking crew. Truthfully I don't remember much from September 12 and 13, 2013, but based on the stories I later heard, it's not the sort of shit I should start discussing now.

Let's leave it at this. Whatever information was made known to the public—the incident at my lawyer's office, the fight at the mall, an altercation with Rocko at the studio—those things were just the tip of the iceberg. I was toxic. Operating in full meltdown mode. Things could only end one way. Badly. And when an Atlanta police officer found me wandering down Moreland shortly after midnight on September 14, they did.

ATLANTA POLICE DEPARTMENT

Incident: 132570142
Report Date: 09/14/2013
Officer Name: IVY

12:51 AM

On 09-14-2013, I, Ofc C. Ivy, was dispatched to Moreland Ave. and E. Confederate on a call about an unknown male by the name of Gucci Mane who was bipolar, off his medication, and possibly armed. While en route to the location I was flagged down by an unknown male (later identified as one of Gucci Mane's friends named [REDACTED]) who called police. Mr. [REDACTED] stated that his friend Gucci Mane was walking down the street and didn't take his medicine and that he was acting violent and that he was worried about him, and that he just wants some help for his friend. Mr. [REDACTED] pointed to the male wearing a white shirt and blue jeans and advised that he was the male that he was calling about.

I made contact with the male later identified as Mr. Radric Davis (AKA Gucci man). I informed him who I was, and who I worked for.

At this moment Mr. Davis asked what did I want? I informed him that his friends called the police because they were worried about him and want to get him some help.

While talking to Mr. Davis I could smell the strong odor of marijuana coming from his person and I also observed a bulge which appeared to be a handgun in his right front pocket. I didn't ask any questions because I didn't want to escalate the situation due to him already being irate.

Mr. Radric Davis was yelling that he wanted the police to drive him to his mother's house in Douglasville and that he didn't need anything else from us. Mr. Davis was informed that we could not go out that far but we would call him an ambulance. At this time more officers had arrived on scene to help assist me with Mr. Davis. Mr. Davis was acting irate by yelling and cursing and threatening police. Once other officers were on scene Mr. Davis got more irate and started to threaten police again and advise that he would shoot us up. Mr. Davis also stated to police that we were gay-ass officers and that we were "homos" trying to fuck him and that we must like men. At this time Mr. Davis was arrested for disorderly conduct and searched incident to the arrest.

While searching Mr. Davis, I located a clear plastic baggie containing suspected marijuana and a loaded black .40 Cal Glock handgun from Mr. Davis's right jean pocket. My supervisor, Sgt. Mitchell (unit 1694), had arrived on scene along with Grady EMS. At this time Grady decided to sedate Mr. Davis based on his behavior and the fact that he has been off his medication. Grady EMS gave Mr. Davis a shot in the left arm to calm him down. At this time Mr. Davis was escorted over to a Grady EMS stretcher so he could be transported to the hospital. While trying to get Mr. Davis onto the stretcher it took several officers and Grady EMS personnel to restrain Mr. Davis. Mr. Davis was administered another dose of medicine by Grady EMS and transported to Grady Hospital.

When we arrived to the hospital Mr. Davis was removed from the ambulance and escorted inside the hospital, where he was checked in and escorted to his room. Mr. Davis was charged with, (Disorderly conduct 16-11-39), (Felon in poss. of firearm 16-11-131), (Carrying concealed weapon 16-11-126), (Poss. of controlled substance 16-13-30(J2), (carrying concealed weapon without license 16-11-126(A), and he also had an active warrant out of Fulton County SO, Warrant #13SC118228, date of warrant 09-13-13. There were no injuries reported from the arrestee while in police custody.

XXI

UNITED STATES OF AMERICA V. RADRIC DAVIS

I'd been brought to Grady Hospital for psychiatric evaluation after my arrest. By the time I sobered up and the sedatives wore off I was in DeKalb County Jail. The way the staff was looking at me, I knew I must have come in there like a man possessed.

I took in my surroundings. There was something different about this room. It felt emptier than the typical DeKalb County cell. Intentionally. There were no sheets on my mattress. The blanket was so stiff. Two nurses peered into my cell and walked away.

This is the mental health floor. You're on suicide watch. These people think you're a psychotic lunatic.

•

"Keyshia," I mumbled through the phone a few hours later. "I'm in jail. Can you come get me?"

"You want me to come get you after everything you said to me?"

"Babe, I'm sorry. I don't know what's wrong with me."

The details of my arrest were still a blur, but I did remember that when I got arraigned I was told I had a cash bond of $130,000. That meant as soon as Keyshia got here and put my bond money up, I was getting out of here.

"Okay," she said. "I'll come."

But Keyshia didn't come.

•

I didn't sleep that night. I couldn't. I knew what was coming.

My mind had been warning me withdrawal was on the way, but it was my body that let me know it had arrived. This was not a mental craving for lean. I was familiar with that feeling. This was dope sickness.

My body was starving for lean like it was food. Screaming for it. I was in terrible pain—stomach cramps, sweats, shakes, vomiting, and diarrhea—alone in my cell.

As I sat on the toilet trembling, breathing heavy, my insides emptying out of me, I hung my head. I closed my eyes and wondered if I'd ever felt pain anywhere close to this.

The extradition from Miami to Fulton County in '05. You were shackled in chains on that bus for two days straight.

I remembered how I got through that. How Big Cat had seen a look of defeat on my face as I was escorted out of the FBI office. How he told me to keep my head up. I remembered how his words carried me through that bus ride and so many other hard times in the years that followed.

I remembered that as low as my lows had gotten, I always

had faith in myself. That I always knew if I could get past those temporary moments, eventually I'd be up again. Jail couldn't beat me. Lean couldn't beat me. No situation could beat me. I was the only one who could beat me.

I lifted my head. I opened my eyes. I'd made it through another round on the toilet.

I was still in the middle of opiate withdrawal. Still exhausted and somehow wide awake. Still aching. Still sweating. Still angry. Still anxious. Still alone. But I wasn't hopeless. I was going to get through this.

•

A few days later I'd made it through the worst of withdrawal but the shits weren't letting up. I'd been here a few days and spent more time sitting on the toilet than I had in years. I needed to see me a doctor. Something was seriously wrong.

"What is going on with me?" I asked a nurse.

"You've been using an opiate for a long time, Mr. Davis," she said bluntly. "As a result of that your metabolism has slowed considerably. You've been constipated. Your body has been retaining everything. Now you're losing that weight."

The fucking lean. *That's* why my stomach had gotten so fat.

•

Tweets from September 22, 2013

11:04 a.m.
Woke up the other day out this hospital bed & I'm so embarrassed & ashamed of my behavior that was brought to my attention. (Cont)

11:05 a.m.

I just wanna man up right now & take this time to apologize to my family, friends, the industry & most of all my fans. I'm SORRY! (Cont)

11:06 a.m.

I've been drinking lean for 10 plus years & I must admit it has destroyed me. I wanna be the first rapper to admit (Cont)

11:08 a.m.

I'm addicted to lean & that shit ain't no joke. I can barely remember all the things I've done & said. However there's no excuse (Cont)

11:10 a.m.

I'm currently incarcerated but I will be going to rehab because I need help. I wanna thank everyone that has stood by me (Cont)

11:11 a.m.

during this difficult time. Please keep me in your prayers. #GUWOP

11:31 a.m.

I wanna personally apologize to birdman ross & drake. Dem my niggas. I 100% regret my words & actions.

11:59 a.m.

Wrote sum new hard shit can't wait to get out dis hell hole so y'all can hear dis shit

12:04 p.m.

Keyshia Dior Kaoir I'm sorry. Please forgive me.

•

"Why the fuck haven't you come down here and bonded me out yet?" I screamed at Keyshia through the phone. It had been nearly two weeks since my arrest and I was still in the same DeKalb County isolation cell.

Keyshia had good reason to not want to help me out. I'd gone crazy on her, first privately on the phone when she'd tried to talk me off the ledge and then on Twitter. But that wasn't why Keyshia hadn't come to bond me out. She'd taken every one of my phone calls since my arrest. Her phone bill was ridiculous from all my collect calls. Despite everything, she still wanted to help me. But Keyshia couldn't get me out of jail.

I had holds. One in Fulton County from my pending assault case from March and another one in DeKalb County for a probation violation. But nobody had said anything to me about these holds since my arraignment, so I'd been sitting there waiting, thinking I was about to get out any minute now. The reason I was still so aggressive and agitated was that I hadn't started the process of mentally adjusting to being locked down again.

That process began on September 27, two weeks after my arrest, when I was sentenced to six months in DeKalb County for violating my probation.

Three days after that I was transferred to Fulton County Jail, where my bond had been revoked from my March arrest. As part of the routine intake procedure they weighed me when I was booked at Fulton County. I couldn't believe it when I stepped on the scale: 240 pounds. I was 265 when they weighed me at Grady Hospital. I'd lost twenty-five pounds in two and a half weeks.

•

When I was transferred back to DeKalb County later that week I was allowed to return to general population.

I now had a court date set for November, and while I still didn't know exactly what I was facing, things weren't looking good. This wasn't going to be another three- or six-month situation. The six months on the probation violation I'd just received was only the beginning. They hadn't even gotten to these new charges yet.

- Carrying a concealed weapon
- Possession of a firearm by a convicted felon
- Disorderly conduct for safety
- Possession of 1 oz. or less of marijuana

They were just getting started.

•

That was when I made a decision. As long as I was here I was going to put my energy into getting more of this weight off. It felt good dropping those twenty-five pounds but I had a long way to go. It wasn't that I wanted to walk out of jail all brolic. That look had never appealed to me. But I did care about my appearance and I'd always fancied myself a dresser. With the way my stomach had gotten, for years I hadn't been able to fit into a lot of the clothes I wanted to wear.

I started with a run up and down a flight of steps. It was all I could do and I was out of breath. Then I ran up and down twice. Then three times. The next day I did five. A week later I did twenty. Very quickly the routine became like another addiction to me and between that and barely eating the snack food they serve in county jail, the pounds started falling right off. I wasn't the only one who noticed.

> *You looking good, Gucci.*
> *Your skin looks a lot better, Gucci.*
> *You talking better, bro.*

I looked different from the man in my September mug shot. And I felt different. Sharper. Stronger. More at ease. The exercise was helping me deal with stress. I wanted to push myself harder, transform myself further. When I did get out, whenever that was, I wanted to be able to go on tour and have the energy to put on a show for my fans. I wanted to be able to keep up with a hectic schedule without falling apart. I wanted to look good doing it. I wanted Keyshia to lose her mind when she came to pick me up. When that would be was out of my control, but I could control whether I was ready for that moment when it came. So I kept running up and down those steps.

●

On November 19, 2013, I was indicted by a federal grand jury on two counts of being a felon in possession of a firearm. My case had gotten picked up by the US Attorney's office. Alongside the ATF and the Atlanta Police Department, they were going to prosecute it on a federal level as part of something they had going on called the Violent Repeat Offender Program.

"The indictment charges that on two separate occasions, this defendant, a convicted felon, threatened individuals, including the police and his attorney, with a gun," said US Attorney Sally Quillian Yates. "This is how people get hurt, and we are committed to ensuring convicted felons not have guns."

"When offenders such as this use firearms to threaten individuals, including law enforcement officers sworn to protect our community, ATF takes this very seriously," added ATF Special Agent in Charge Christopher Shaefer. "ATF remains on the front line of preventing violent crime along with our law enforcement partners and will continue to pursue those who violate the law, regardless of their celebrity status."

"The Atlanta Police Department has made it a priority to take violent repeat offenders off our city streets and see that they are held responsible for their actions. We are thankful for the cooperation with our partner agencies, especially the US Attorney's office, in bringing Mr. Davis to justice. We cannot tolerate convicted felons ignoring the law by carrying firearms and endangering our citizens," said Atlanta Police Chief George Turner.

This was bad. Very bad. I had two weapons charges. One from when I got arrested by the Kroger on Moreland and one from the incident the day before at my lawyer's office. Each of those charges carried up to ten years in prison. Then I still had my open assault case in Fulton County to deal with. Between the feds and the state of Georgia I was facing thirty-five years.

Fuck.

I started doing the math. Thirty-five years meant my life would essentially be over. But what if they didn't give me thirty-five. What if they settled for ten? Then my career would be over. And my story would be another one of wasted talent. It was time to make an example out of Gucci Mane, and I'd never been so afraid.

•

On the Friday after Thanksgiving I was transferred to the Robert A. Deyton Detention Facility in Lovejoy, Georgia. This was a holdover prison, a privately owned facility that made its money housing people awaiting the outcome of their federal cases. Most of the guys in there were Puerto Rican and a lot of them had never even been to the States before being flown out here after catching their cases. The place had a lot of Puerto Ricans and blacks fighting, but none of that ever involved me. I fucked with the Puerto Ricans and they fucked with me.

County jail was no picnic, but after a few bids I did have some familiarity with the place. In the feds I felt much more removed from the people and the world I knew. But there was one face I recognized at the Robert A. Deyton Detention Facility: Doo Dirty, my old partner from Savannah.

Doo Dirty had been here a few years now, trying to fight a twenty-year sentence he'd received after pleading guilty on drug conspiracy charges. The DEA had learned of his activities on a wiretap and after getting a few niggas to roll on him, his name was at the top of a forty-five-person indictment, accused of being behind the distribution of two hundred bricks of blow throughout the Savannah area.

I hadn't seen Doo Dirty in years and when he found out I'd ended up in Lovejoy he tried to get himself moved into my unit. He ended up in the one adjacent to mine. He and I caught up one day, talking through the door that separated our pods. We talked old times and had a few laughs.

It was good to see him, but after that first reunion we wouldn't speak again. Soon after I was seen talking to him I was told by someone that Doo Dirty was a rat. He'd snitched on the Mexicans he dealt with after he got pinched. I had no bad feelings toward him but his decisions made it impossible for us to reconcile our friendship. There was no way I was wearing the jacket he had on and I couldn't let inmates think I condoned what he did, because truth is I didn't.

Whether it's the feds, state prison, county jail, or the drunk tank, the quickest way to endanger yourself behind bars is to get people thinking you're a rat or are even friends with one. When you let that happen you've taken a very serious risk. And where I was going, the consequences of those risks were unlike anything I'd ever known.

XXII

MAVERICK

I would always get a little stir-crazy when I was locked up, but this time was especially challenging. I was in a facility an hour outside of Atlanta where I hardly knew anyone and I didn't know how long I was going to be there. I was keeping busy with the exercise but I needed something else. I needed to find a way to be involved with the world beyond this prison. I needed my name to still be in the mix.

For all of my problems, a lack of music was not one of them. The Brick Factory was now closed. I'd had everything moved out of the studio and into a storage unit across the street. But I had hard drives full of the unreleased songs I'd made there as well as a mountain of older shit from Patchwerk and other studios. So I kept releasing tapes from behind bars, delegating the task of rifling through the archives to Sean. He and I worked together to put out new projects from what we had in the vaults. Sean worked hard—I think he put out nearly twenty-five mixtapes while I was locked up.

The releases accomplished the goal of keeping my name active. And they were bringing in some money. But none of those songs would blow up in my absence like they had in years past. Still, somehow the legend of Gucci seemed to be growing stronger by the day.

This was because one by one, all the young guns I'd taken under my wing at the Brick Factory were blowing up. My fingerprints were all over their music and they were making their reverence for me known.

Migos, whom I'd handed off to Pee and Coach, had gotten themselves a deal with Todd and Lyor at 300. Metro Boomin had gone from a freshman at Morehouse to having a platinum plaque to his name. Peewee and Dolph were doing their thing. And then there was Thug. The one I signed to Brick Squad on a whim had become the hottest up-and-coming artist in the rap game.

There was now a bidding war for Thug's contract. He wanted to go work with Birdman and Lil Wayne. The media blew that situation up to be bigger than it was because I never had a problem with it. Me being pissed at Thug or Bird would be like Michael Vick blaming the Falcons for drafting Matt Ryan when he got locked up. At the end of the day everyone's got to do what's best for themselves. When all was said and done Thug signed a deal at 300 too, which I was pleased about because I knew he would be in good hands with Todd. And I was compensated for my role in his career with an amount I felt was fair. Nothing else to it.

Listen, I shined the light on Thug and he and I got to make a ton of great music together, but his talent and work ethic got him to where he's at. Whether it was with 1017 or Cash Money or 300, I always wanted to see him go as far as he could go. I never wanted to hinder him. And if for some reason shit didn't work out for him, I couldn't let myself be the cause of that. The idea that Thug could have blown up but Gucci had him locked up in a contract, that didn't sit right with me. I felt like I'd been in that situation myself.

When I was in the streets I did a lot of dirt. A lot of slimy, shameful shit. But I take pride in that I never gypped someone in the music business. Somehow I was able to draw a line there. When someone trusted me with their career, I valued that trust and always did my best to deliver on what I told them I was going to do for them.

Even when shit got sticky I was rooting for those guys. The rap game is a business I take seriously, but I take a liking to these artists personally too. We were all basically living together at the Brick Factory. We got a lot of work done, but there was a lot of gambling and watching ball games and enjoying each other's company too. So it's never just business. Sometimes situations need to get figured out, but I was always rooting for Thug. I was always rooting for Migos. For Scooter, for Dolph, for Peewee. No matter what happened I was always rooting for Waka and OJ to win. I still am. That's the truth.

Even if my lane was just to get these guys hot, make a little money together, and then let them go do their own thing else-where, that's not a bad lane to be in. Because I want the next generation—the young niggas *after* Thug and Migos—to see the role I played in those artists' successes and want to come rock with me too.

And they did. As I bided my time in the feds, waiting on developments on my cases, I started hearing about the next generation of kids coming up. Fetty Wap, iLoveMakonnen, 21 Savage, Kodak Black, Lil Yachty, Dreezy. I hadn't had a hand in any of their careers nor had I ever met them, but they were out here screaming "Free Guwop," putting out music in my honor and calling me their biggest influence in interviews.

•

Young people are searching for the truth. It's why little kids say some of the rudest shit sometimes. Like they'll tell somebody they're fat or ugly. Most of the time those people are ugly as hell. The youngins just don't know yet that they're not supposed to say those kinds of things. As they get older they learn to put on the mask and pretend.

Those kids gravitated toward me because I was the closest thing to an established artist who said what he meant and meant what he said. That's called authenticity. I don't walk around acting hard but I do go anywhere that I want. Any club, any mall, any block, any hood. They see that I'm not hiding behind my music and they respect that. They like it that I'll show up to T.I.'s party looking like a walking lick. They like that I'll go to Macon and perform "The Truth." They like that they can catch me riding around Zone 6 in a Phantom with no security. Part of being young is being brave. And part of being brave is being a little brazen, being a little reckless. It's safe to say I've always been that.

When they meet other established artists and it's not the same, that can be hard for them. If they're smart, they can figure out how to work industry relationships to their benefit. If they're not, they'll get used as pawns. For niggas like Thug and Peewee, coming from the world they came from, it's not easy to flip a switch and all of a sudden be able to play the fake political games of the music business. Those boys were really in the streets. As much as Thug may have wanted to make it in music, he could never have been an errand boy for some big-name rapper waiting for his boss to put him on. He's not a yes man. That shit is not in him.

I'm honored by the credit I've gotten for introducing these boys to the world, but having them around helped me too. I may be considered the godfather of this trap shit but I was never the elder statesman at the Brick Factory, walking around with my chest out, acting like I could teach the youngsters a thing or two. If anything, it was the other way around.

Keeping Thug and Peewee and Dolph and Migos around kept me connected to what was going on in the streets and what was resonating with the youth. I was getting older and richer and as much as I hate to admit it, the shit I was rapping—my reference points, my slang, my whole swag—could have easily become outdated. But these boys were still there. They were rapping about what they didn't even have yet, what they were aspiring to. I fed off their hunger. It made me hungry. Their excitement excited me. It brought me back to when I was in their shoes and that made my music better. I've been blessed to work with a lot of great artists in my career, but I never had more fun making music than when I was at the Brick Factory with those boys.

The other reason nobody broke artists in Atlanta the way I did was because my method didn't make much sense on paper. An established recording artist, a multimillionaire, hanging out with twenty-year-old street niggas in a studio off Moreland in East Atlanta every day, that shit doesn't add up. But for me it did. Because I always made myself accessible. No matter how much money I made or how famous I became, I was never able to withdraw myself from that world. That's something that's given me the reputation I have, but it's something that's had its drawbacks. Big ones.

I didn't get into music to make enough money so I could go sit in some mansion alone, isolated from the people and places I enjoyed being around. I got into it to make a good living doing something I enjoyed doing. And to me, going to the studio every now and then so I can put out an album a year and tour, that's not living. That's not me. That's not how I operate.

I knew when I got out I needed to make big changes. Still, I don't think I could ever live like that.

XXIII

CON AIR

On May 13, 2014, I pleaded guilty to one count of possession of a firearm by a convicted felon. The government agreed to drop the second count so long as I waived my rights to that loaded .45 the police found in my lawyer's office that day.

I was happy to let the feds keep the guns. They could keep the bullets too. No problem. The rest of the plea deal was a harder pill to swallow.

After months of negotiations between my lawyers and the US Attorney's office, we settled on a sentence of thirty-nine months. Three years, three months. That was a whole lot of time to spend in federal prison. But what could I do? When the feds got you, they pretty much got you. I sure as hell wasn't about to try my luck at trial. They'd give me the whole twenty if I did that. Thirty-nine months was not going to be easy, but it wasn't twenty years.

I could survive thirty-nine months, and it wouldn't be too late for me to salvage my career when I got out.

"Mr. Davis, you heard the summary coming from the assistant US attorney and you heard what the court has said," said US District Judge Steve Jones. "Do you agree with what the assistant US attorney is saying the evidence would show if this case went to trial?"

"Yes."

"Do you agree with that?"

"Yes, sir, I agree."

"Are you in fact guilty as alleged in count one of the indictment?"

"Yes."

"Now, Mr. Davis, a lot has been said this morning. A lot of questions have been asked of you this morning. Is there anything that the court has asked you or said to you that you wish for me to clarify?"

"I totally understand everything."

"Is there anything your attorneys have said that you disagree with during the course of this hearing?"

"No, sir."

"At this time the court finds the defendant understands the charges and the consequences of his plea of guilty. I have observed the defendant during this proceeding. He does not appear to be under the influence of any substance that might affect his judgment or actions in any manner. The court finds that the offer of the plea of guilty to count one of the indictment has a factual basis, and is free of any coercive influence of any kind, is voluntarily made with full knowledge of the charge against him and the consequence of his plea.

———

"I further find that the defendant is competent to understand these proceedings and to enter a knowing plea of guilty. I find that there has been no promises of any kind made to him by anyone except as incorporated in the plea agreement as set out here in open court.

"It is hereby ordered that the plea of guilty of the defendant to count one of the indictment is accepted and entered. Mr. Davis, you are hereby adjudged guilty of count one of the indictment."

•

In the fall I pleaded guilty to the incident at Harlem Nights with the soldier. For that I received another three years. But I'd get to serve my two sentences concurrently. There would be no going back to Fulton County. Ever. But I was going somewhere. The detention facility in Lovejoy was for inmates awaiting outcomes of their cases, and my cases were now resolved. It was time for me to go to federal prison.

At my sentencing my lawyer requested I be sent somewhere on the West Coast, away from the distractions of home as I kept working toward rehabilitating myself. Specifically he'd asked that I be sent to FCI Taft in California or FCI Sheridan in Oregon, two minimum-security facilities that offered residential drug and alcohol programs.

I'd now been sober for a year and I already knew I would never drink lean or use any type of drugs again. I'd always been a strong-minded person and I'd made up my mind. Some people can put those substances in their body and be totally fine. More power to them. I don't judge anyone who does. I'm just not one of those people. I'd finally realized that. It wasn't only that I'd learned my limits; I really had no desire to go back. I had no cravings. It was the opposite. I now associated drugs with my lowest moments, with prison, with all the time I'd cost myself and others. I didn't know what else I could learn at one of these drug treatment programs, but going to a minimum-security facility sounded good to me.

The judge had been receptive to my lawyer's request but unfortunately my destination wasn't his call to make. That decision belonged to the Federal Bureau of Prisons. And the Bureau of Prisons had other plans for me.

I was given no heads-up of the transfer ahead of time. It was the middle of the night when they came to my cell in Lovejoy and told me it was time to go.

Me and a few other inmates were bused to a secluded airstrip nearby where an airplane awaited us. Surrounding the plane were US Marshals, all of whom were carrying shotguns or rifles. We were lined up and patted down. Then, cuffed, shackled, and chained at the belly, I boarded the plane, where several dozen inmates were already on board from a prior stop.

A slave ship of the skies.

Hours later the plane touched down at FTC Oklahoma City, a holdover facility where all federal inmates stop before their final destination. After the intake process I was immediately sent to solitary confinement.

My second night there I was shaken out of my bed by a rumble. Earthquake. It was my first and it scared the hell out of me, even more than getting caught in a tornado during that flight to Houston in '09. It was like this prison had grown itself a pair of legs and started jumping all over the place.

Two weeks later I was on a bus, staring out the window into an endless stream of countryside. I was headed five hours north, to the United States Penitentiary in Leavenworth County, Kansas.

But this would be another pit stop. I now knew my final destination, the USP in Terre Haute, but there had been an outbreak of tuberculosis there and the place was on lockdown. I'd spend a month and a half in Kansas before the quarantine was lifted. Then, two months after I'd first left Georgia, I arrived at my new home in Bumblefuck, Indiana.

The United States Penitentiary in Terre Haute was not like the federal facilities I'd just come from in Lovejoy, Leavenworth, or Oklahoma City. And it was nothing like county jail. A maximum-security federal penitentiary is different. There's a certain level of violence in any correctional facility but here it was intrinsic. It lived in the concrete walls. In the steel doors. It was always hanging in the air.

I was surrounded by lifers and men on death row. The Aryan Brotherhood, MS-13, Crips, Bloods, mob bosses, terrorists. This was where the Oklahoma City bomber got the lethal injection. A few months after I got there I saw on the news that they were sending the Boston Marathon Bomber here to await his death. They call it Guantánamo North. I knew I'd fucked up but I didn't belong here. It reminded me of when they had me a few doors down from Brian Nichols in Fulton County. This has to be a mistake.

But I'm a man wherever you land me. Regardless of where that is or who is in front of me, there's a standard that I hold myself to and a certain level of respect I expect to be treated with. When I first got to the USP there was a whole bunch of hoopla about my arrival, because for somebody doing life, having a celebrity in general population is exciting. It's something to write home about. So I had to make it clear I wasn't there for any dick-riding groupie shit or to be a part of the world they had going on here. I was here to do my time, protect myself, and then leave.

That ain't even on some tough-guy shit. Hell, I was scared too. When people talk about prison you often hear them talk about wolves and sheep. To survive you've got to be a wolf. But here it was all wolves. Tough guys were getting killed here every day. You could be Gucci. You could be Al Capone. It didn't matter because they'd kill your ass the same. This was a place full of men with nothing to lose. There were nights I lay in bed and I could hear the sound of someone sharpening shanks. I prayed those knives weren't meant for me.

XXIV

EL CHAPO'S ESCAPE

Prison is time. I tried to use the time to better myself. I kept up with the exercise, taking part in the workout classes they offered along with my own daily routine. I lost nearly eighty pounds in total. Keyshia was putting money on my books so I was able to work the cafeteria staff and eat a little better than the slop they were serving in there.

I followed the changes I'd made to my body by working to strengthen my mind. I was devouring books. A lot of self-help, inspirational stuff. Tony Robbins. Deepak Chopra. Malcolm Gladwell. James Allen. The biographies of Pimp C. and Jimi Hendrix. Mike Tyson's autobiography.

I got an MP3 player from the prison commissary and started downloading instrumentals from the BOP's music server. Then I got back to writing raps, something I hadn't done much of since my incarceration. I'd been too jaded. Resentful. Mad at the industry. Mad at the world. Mad at every person I could point my finger at and blame my misfortunes on. For so long I'd felt like I'd been dealt a bad hand.

But prison is a humbling experience. It was hell in there and over time that made me start to appreciate all my blessings on the outside. I had a damn good life waiting for me.

I had a career that people still cared about, maybe now more than ever before. And I had so many things I still wanted to do. I wanted a platinum record. I wanted to tour the world. I wanted to direct and act in more movies. I wanted to have my own clothing line. I wanted to discover and groom more talent and become the next Berry Gordy. It wasn't too late. And all of that was still attainable. It was all within reach.

I had Keyshia, my first real love. The first woman I ever wanted to bring to a red carpet and let the world know this was my lady. Not just "This is Gucci's girl and she's pretty" but as my partner, my equal. She held me down the whole time I was locked up and showed me what it means to have somebody you can truly count on. I wanted to be able to return the favor.

I had Bam, my little boy. He needed me. Before I got sent to Indiana he came to see me in Lovejoy and that visit was not easy. I could see him trying to make sense of why there was glass between us, why we were talking through a phone, why his daddy couldn't have his hands on him. He was too young to understand it, but he knew it wasn't supposed to be like this.

I can't get taken away from them again.

What good is fame if I can't enjoy it? What good is money if I can't spend it? How long will Keyshia stick around if I keep going back to jail? Or if I'm so gone off the lean I'm having seizures? Or if I'm taking chances that could end with me getting shot up and paralyzed? Or killed?

I can't put myself through this shit anymore.

For all the promising things I had waiting for me outside this prison there was just as much danger waiting if I wasn't on point. I wasn't invincible. I was hearing about other artists overdosing on drugs. I was hearing about Bankroll Fresh and Chinx Drugz and Doe B, young niggas who were on their way to making it and getting killed in some street shit. Beasley, who'd helped me set up my studio and was like a sister to me, had gotten shot and killed outside of her restaurant right on Bouldercrest in front of her kids.

Unlike a lot of the guys in this place, I was getting another chance. My last one. I couldn't drop the ball again. I needed to do more than pray. I needed to make better decisions.

•

On the morning of July 12, 2015, I walked into the common room where a bunch of inmates were gathered around the TV. They seemed excited. Joaquín "El Chapo" Guzmán, the head of Mexico's notorious Sinaloa cartel, had broken out again. This guy was a damn escape artist. His partners dug a mile-long tunnel that went under the prison and up to his cell. All Chapo had to do was go down the hole in his shower stall. A dirt bike was at the bottom, waiting for him. He did it again. Unbelievable. Legendary.

Now *I* was excited. Chapo was my guy. I'd done a song in his tribute years back. I'd always had an interest in the stories of the narco kingpins, just as a fan of history. Chapo, Escobar, Griselda Blanco, the Félix Brothers. I fucked with all of 'em.

My mind was off to the races. What move could I pull with this news? I'd already used my ten minutes of phone time that morning, but maybe tomorrow I could do an "El Chapo" free-style on the phone and have Sean record it on the other end. Or maybe he could just put some old songs together, get a dope cover made, and we could drop an *El Chapo* mixtape. At the very least my Twitter should have something to say about this.

Later in the day I was typing away on CorrLinks, the Bureau of Prison's e-mail system for inmates. I'd spent all day thinking up ideas for the *El Chapo* mixtape and we needed to move on it ASAP before someone else did. Halfway through writing that e-mail I stopped.

I wanted to leave this place as soon as possible. I'd spoken to my lawyer a few days earlier. He was in the middle of negotiating with the BOP to get my release date sorted out. We were aiming for an early release and for me to serve the end of my sentence on house arrest in Georgia. Maybe glorifying El Chapo's escape from behind bars wasn't going to help my case there. Maybe this just wasn't the best idea after all.

I logged out of CorrLinks and went back up to my cell so I could change into my exercise clothes. I had a workout class that was starting up shortly. I wanted to be ready for it.

•

In February 2016 we got everything sorted out with the BOP. For a while my release date had been listed as March 2017, because they weren't giving me credit for time served prior to my sentencing. I knew eventually we'd get that fixed.

My new release date was September 20, 2016, but I would get to come home in May and serve the last four months on house arrest. Just three more months.

I couldn't wait to get home. To see Keyshia. To see Bam. To

see my brother. Mother dearest. The rest of my family and my close partners.

I couldn't wait to get back to work. With the help of Todd I'd patched things up with Atlantic and they were ready to roll out the red carpet for my comeback album. They wouldn't have to wait long for it. I couldn't wait to get back to work. I'd gone through all the songs I'd written and I knew which ones I wanted for this album. They just needed beats. So I told Zay and Mike Will that I needed them as soon as I came home. They were ready to join me on house arrest and lock in. The *New York Times* wanted to come interview me. *Fader* magazine wanted me on their cover. *XXL* wanted me on their cover. The clothing brand Supreme wanted me for their fall collection and Harmony was going to shoot the video for it. I was nearly finished writing my memoir. Believe it or not, I even had a couple of book deal offers on the table.

There was a lot to look forward to and I couldn't wait to show every person who counted me out how mistaken they were. That my story wasn't one to be pitied or laughed at but one to be inspired by. But I still had to prove that. Along with all the great things waiting for me out there was my biggest test. Keeping sober and working out and not letting this prison swallow me up had been the easy part. Soon I'd have to take my real stand.

My father used to say that if you keep looking back you're going to trip going forward. That in life, sometimes you reach a fork in the road and you have to make a decision. Which direction will it be? Left or right?

To be firm in that decision you can't keep looking back. You have to make peace with the past. It doesn't happen overnight. It takes time for wounds to heal. But I had time. Three years to think about it all. The relationships that matter most. The ones that have run their course. The mistakes I can't afford to make again. My strengths. My shortcomings. My limits. The way I've got to respond when times get tough again because tough times are a part of life. It's how you bounce back from those moments that make you who you are.

Three years to replay things in my head over and over and over until I stopped replaying them. Until I just let them go.

If you keep lookin' back you gon' trip going forward.

I've taken heed of that. To start a new chapter you've got to turn the page on the last one. Still, every now and then I do think it's okay to stop and look back, just for a moment, before continuing on your way. Especially when it's a hell of a story.

ACKNOWLEDGMENTS

Gucci Mane would like to thank:

My wife, my brother Victor Davis, and all my fans.

Neil Martinez-Belkin would like to thank:

Gucci. What a journey it has been. Thank you for trusting me to help you tell your story. Such an honor. There are many things I respect and admire you for, my favorite might be your willingness to give anybody a shot. I'm forever grateful for mine.

My agent Robert Guinsler of Sterling Lord Literistic. Thank you for taking a chance on me and this book. For finding a home for it and sticking by me every step of the way.

My editor, Stuart Roberts, and the talented team at Simon & Schuster. Your entry into this project was a breath of fresh air. You guys were what this book needed when it needed it. Let's do it again sometime.

I am indebted to so many of Gucci's family members and friends for their contributions to this book, most of all Keyshia Ka'oir, Victor Davis, Brandon Putmon, Amanda Dudley, and De-meria Evans. Thank you for taking my calls and visits and always helping connect the dots.

Thank you to everyone who took the time to share their Gucci memories with me: Zaytoven, Mike WiLL Made It, Todd Moscowitz, Amina Diop, Sean Paine, Suge Sheppard, Fatboi, Kori Anders, Shawty Redd, Drumma Boy, Honorable C.N.O.T.E., DJ Drama, DJ Holiday, DJ Burn One, DJ Ace, DJ Mad Linx, Young Dolph, Jacob York, Johnny Cabbel, Harmony Korine, Caveman, Throwback, and Ralph Dudley.

Thank you to Geordie Wood, Zach Wolfe, Cam Kirk, Diwang Valdez, Quang Le, and Gunner Stahl, for blessing this book with your photographs and for your dedication to documenting culture in such striking ways.

Thank you to the staff at Atlantic Records for getting involved in this effort and supporting this book's release.

To Benjamin Meadows-Ingram. Thank you for shepherding me throughout this process and for tossing me several alley-oops along the way for no reason other than that's the type of person you are. I'm inspired by your character and I'll pay it forward.

To Adam Fleischer. Thank you for putting me on and being the first person to ever put a dollar in my pocket for something I wrote. I never forgot it.

To the rest of the *XXL* gang: Carl Chery, Ralph Bristout, Tzvi Twersky, Eric Diep, Dan Buyanovsky, Sean Ryon, Manny Maduakolam, Jaeki Cho, Emily Cappiello, Mark Lelinwalla, Alex Gale, Vernon Coleman, Jayson Rodriguez, Mariel Concepcion, and Josh Clutter. Thank you for being friends and mentors as I was finding my footing in this industry.

Thank you to every writer and editor I've had the pleasure of working with and learning from as well as those whose work inspired me to think differently and step my game up.

To Paul. Thank you for supporting my writing from an early

age and for all your words of wisdom and encouragement as I pursued this.

To my family and friends. Thank you for cheering me on as I chased a dream. I am one lucky guy.

To my parents. Thank you for teaching me about this world and giving me the compass I navigate it with.

And to Danielle. Thanks for being you and loving me. I love you.

ILLUSTRATION CREDITS

INDEX

INDEX

ABOUT THE AUTHOR

Gucci Mane, born Radric Delantic Davis, is a critically acclaimed, platinum-selling recording artist. He has released eight studio albums and dozens of mixtapes. He lives in Atlanta, Georgia, with his wife, Keyshia Ka'oir. *The Autobiography of Gucci Mane* is his first book.

www.guccimaneonline.com
Twitter: @gucci1017
Instagram: @laflare1017
Snapchat: GuwopSnap
Facebook: Gucci Mane

Neil Martinez-Belkin is the former music editor at *XXL* Magazine and has written extensively about contemporary hip-hop with a regional focus on Atlanta. He lives in Boston.

Twitter: @neil_mb